Although Jesus gave us a mandate to [...]
ual. Keep this book handy. It will [...]
invest in others.

—ROBBY GALLATY, senior pastor, Long Hollow Baptist Church;
author, *Growing Up* and *Rediscovering Discipleship*

Reading this book was like having a conversation with friends and authors I respect. You are going to find it very useful with your colleagues and members of your congregation.

—BILL HULL, senior leader, The Bonhoeffer Project; author,
Jesus Christ Disciplemaker and *Conversion and Discipleship*

Presents a simple yet powerful framework for considering the contexts within which discipleship happens. It will help individuals to live more balanced lives and church leaders to be more strategic.

—TODD WILSON, founder and director,
Exponential Conference; author, *More*

Bobby and Alex have done a great job explaining that discipleship happens best and only in relationship. Not only do these guys write about it; they live it out as well.

—JIM PUTMAN, pastor; founder, Relational
Discipleship Network; author, *DiscipleShift*

This book is a winner. Biblically substantial and rich in practical suggestions, it's a very welcome addition to the growing writings on the essential area of discipleship.

—ALAN HIRSCH, founder, Future Travelers and 100Movements;
author, *The Forgotten Ways* and *The Faith of Leap*

I plan to add this book to my equipping toolbelt because I'm confident it will aid the church in fulfilling the Everyday Commission Jesus has given us.

—JEFF VANDERSTELT, visionary leader of the
Soma Family of Churches; author, *Saturate*

The words of Jesus in Matthew 28, "Go make disciples," mean, "As you are going about living life, make disciple-makers." Read this book, find your fit, and get on with doing it.

—DAVE BUEHRING, president, Lionshare; author, *A Discipleship Journey*

A fresh and needed perspective. Bobby and Alex make discipleship more understandable and tangible for every Christian, in every kind of church. Useful and encouraging.

—DR. KENNON VAUGHAN, lead pastor,
Harvest Church; founder, Downline Ministries

Looking at five contexts for relationships, Bobby and Alex show us how to leverage each for fruitful discipling. This book is one that you will come back to over and over again.

—DR. DANN SPADER, founder, Sonlife and Global Youth Initiative;
author, *Four Chair Discipling* and *Walking as Jesus Walked*

Developing a praxis of discipleship that brings the best thought of how people actually communicate, belong, and grow is genius. This book will bring your discipleship program to life.

—JOSEPH R. MYERS, author,
The Search to Belong and *Organic Community*

Bobby and Alex challenge us to reimagine discipleship in all of life. If you're tired of feeling out of place when it comes to discipleship and evangelism, read this book.

—CAESAR KALINOWSKI, author,
Transformed and *Small Is Big, Slow Is Fast*

I am thankful for what Alex and Bobby have here given the church, and I commend their very fine contribution with all my heart.

—MICHAEL CASSIDY, founder, African Enterprise;
author, *The Church Jesus Prayed For*

As a biblical, practical, and missional treatment of discipleship, this book is guaranteed to give any church leader fresh insight and breakthrough ideas for ministry.

—WILL MANCINI, founder, Auxano Consulting;
author, *God Dreams* and *Church Unique*

Refreshing. Balanced. Biblical. Practical. Thought-provoking. This simple book carries a big punch, from practitioners, not theorists, and has a message we have needed for a long time.

—NEIL COLE, author, *Ordinary Hero*, *Organic Church*, and *Primal Fire*

DISCIPLESHIP That **FITS**

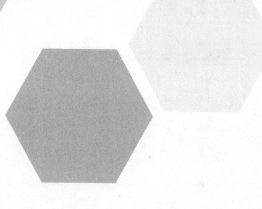

DISCIPLESHIP
That FITS

The Five Kinds of Relationships
God Uses to Help Us Grow

Bobby
Harrington
and Alex
Absalom

ZONDERVAN®

ZONDERVAN

Discipleship That Fits
Copyright © 2016 by Bobby Harrington and Alex Absalom

This title is also available as a Zondervan ebook. Visit www.zondervan.com/ebooks.

Requests for information should be addressed to:

Zondervan, 3900 *Sparks Dr. SE, Grand Rapids, Michigan* 49546

Library of Congress Cataloging-in-Publication Data

Harrington, Bobby, 1958-
    Discipleship that fits : the five kinds of relationships God uses to help us grow /
    Bobby Harrington and Alex Absalom.
        pages   cm
    Includes bibliographical references.
    ISBN 978-0-310-52261-4 (softcover)
    1. Discipling (Christianity) I. Title.
BV4520.H374   2016
253—dc23   2015030233

Published in association with the literary agency of Mark Sweeney and Associates, Bonita Springs, Florida 34135.

Cover design: LUCAS Art and Design
Interior design: Kait Lamphere

Printed in the United States of America

15 16 17 18 19 20 21 22 23 24 25 /DHV/ 15 14 13 12 11 10 9 8 7 6 5 4 3 2 1

From Bobby:
For Ashley and Andrew,
my delightful daughter and her new husband
From Alex:
For my three naughty sons
and my one foxy wife:
in our Jesus adventure, you enrich every context!

CONTENTS

The Transparent Context

The Divine Context

Uniting the Contexts

FOREWORD

JESUS KEPT IT SIMPLE. *Make disciples.* That was the primary command of the Great Commission. It remains the primary responsibility of the local church. Our Savior's call to missions and evangelism is much more than a call to share the gospel with those who do not have it. It is a call to make *disciples* of the nations. It is a call to lead those who do not know Jesus Christ to become fully orbed followers of our King, men and women who know what it means to live for Christ's glory and to advance his kingdom. Disciple making begins by proclaiming the gospel. It continues as new Christians are adopted into a New Testament community of faith, the local church, and taught the implications of living out the gospel. *That* is how the church teaches disciples to obey "all" that Jesus has commanded (Matt. 28:18–20). Evangelism and discipleship are gospel centric and inseparable.

Surprisingly, the church as a whole has not always understood the correlation between evangelism and discipleship. This misunderstanding has given rise to churches that produce large numbers of converts with little depth, converts who could hardly be called disciples of Jesus Christ. These churches are often said to be great at evangelism but poor at discipleship. Conversely, there are also many churches that emphasize great teaching and theological depth but fail to see God use them to bring very many, if any, new believers to faith in Christ. These churches are often said to be great at discipleship but poor at evangelism. Neither pattern, however, reveals churches that practice biblically faithful evangelism and discipleship.

The church's struggles to make and disciple Christians has not been lost on her leadership. In an effort to address contemporary shortcomings in the church's discipleship ministries, numerous authors (including me) have produced a staggering number of resources on the topic in the last few decades. A quick perusal of the topic on Amazon.com reveals almost twenty thousand options! When those resources are added to the number of websites, blog articles, and downloadable sermons on this subject, there are seemingly innumerable alternatives from which church leaders can choose as they seek to lead their churches to greater effectiveness.

To that gargantuan collection of resources, Bobby Harrington and Alex Absalom have added *Discipleship That Fits*. The question arises, Does the church really need *another* book on discipleship? The answer is a resounding yes! Harrington and Absalom offer a refreshing and helpful perspective on this topic and remind us of an often-neglected context for effective disciple making: relationships.

When the gospel is preached, sinners are called to enter into a saving relationship with Jesus Christ. At the same time, the gospel calls us to enter the community of faith for which Christ died: the church. Christianity *happens* in relationships. They are the context in which meaningful spiritual growth takes place. In *Discipleship That Fits*, the authors articulate a helpful and meaningful paradigm through which church leaders can utilize natural, relational dynamics to cultivate a meaningful and biblically faithful discipleship ministry within the local church. Do yourself a favor; buy this book, study this book, and evaluate your church's disciple-making ministries in light of its conclusions. A church that utilizes the approach advocated by Harrington and Absalom cannot help but produce maturing disciples who labor together to advance the kingdom.

—Thom S. Rainer, President and CEO,
LifeWay Christian Resources

ACKNOWLEDGMENTS

NUMEROUS STICKY FINGERS have left their marks on this book, and we are so grateful, since this work would not exist otherwise. Some have inspired us to cook up ideas, others have been in the trenches as we tried to live them, and still others have served to capture and present their essence in these words.

In particular, we are immensely grateful to the whole team at Zondervan, led by our editors Ryan Pazdur and Brian Phipps, who have been patient, encouraging, and diligent in the details of the publishing process. Our gracious and generous agent, Mark Sweeney, also deserves our warm thanks.

On the ideas front, Joseph Myers has been an ongoing fount of out-of-the-normal thinking, and it is an honor to be able to build on his previous work. Many years ago, Anders Michael Hansen first pointed Alex in this direction of thinking, while simultaneously drinking quad espresso and trying to break the speed limit in a golf cart. Most Scandinavians seem to be like that. A special thanks to Kyle Froman for the icons; he has always been a great help to Harpeth Christian Church as a graphic designer. Plenty of other thinkers and practitioners have been a rich blessing along the way, such as Jim Putman, Alan Hirsch, Jeff Vanderstelt, Mick Woodhead, Neil Cole, Mike Breen, Caesar Kalinowski, Dave and Jon Ferguson, Todd Wilson, Hugh Halter, Matt Smay, Bill Hull, KP Yohanan, Francis Chan, Robby Gallaty, Robert Coleman, Dann Spader, and others.

Many thanks to Thom Rainer for the insightful and kind foreword.

He has a wicked sense of humor, and he has been a wise and kind friend to Bobby since the days when Thom served as his doctor of ministry mentor at Southern Seminary. And if you bought this book because you glimpsed his name on the cover and thought it was all by him, apologies.

Bobby is grateful to his son Chad, who helped him with some of the writing, and his wife, Cindy, for all her support. He is also grateful to the leadership at Harpeth Christian Church: David Sanders, Ed Kaeser, Tony Dupree, Mike Shake, Josh Patrick, Michelle Eagle, Kathy Cawley, Alan Garrett, Cam McLaughlin, Aaron Spelzhaus, and Nicky York.

Alex is grateful to Carey Wachtel for tech support, and the amazing team at Rivertree Christian Church in Ohio for five years of collegiality, fun, and experimentation—notably Tammy Jones, Al Dangelo, John Moores, Gary Dolan, Greg Nettle, and Jason Lantz. Special thanks go to all those leaders of Missional Gatherings / GoCommunities / Housechurches / Clusters who, down the years, we have had the privilege of coaching, leading and learning alongside. Thank you for being willing to take the risk to pioneer, and to boldly go and make disciples wherever Jesus takes you. Thank you to Hannah, my idyllic partner in life and ministry: I love watching and learning from you, and I look so much wiser than I really am by being known as your husband. Joel, Samuel, and Isaac, you each make us such a wonderful family with whom to live on mission and never stop taking risks with Jesus. And finally, thank you, Jesus, for your grace, blessings, and sense of humor in letting me be in any way involved in church leadership.

Chapter One

IT'S A JOURNEY

Reimagining Discipleship

Ryan and Ginger are passionate about training the children in their missional community to be disciple makers. A missional community is twenty to fifty people who serve others, build community, and make disciples Their missional community is made up of young families, most with children who are elementary school age. At the start of their gatherings, they share a meal together. Then after everyone has assembled and finished eating (typically between thirty-five and forty-five people total, counting children and adults), thanksgivings are shared around the table. Every person, young and old, is invited to contribute, simply by sharing something from the past week for which they are thankful to God.

Next, a short story from Scripture is read out loud twice to the room. Then parents are told to find a corner in the house, close their Bibles, and retell that same story twice to their children! In response the kids tell it back to them, and then they discuss as a family what God is saying to them out of that passage. Afterward everyone comes back together and a few reports take place.

This time with the families together is followed by small group time. There are groups for men and for women, for the seven- to thirteen-year-olds, and for the three- to six-year-olds. The seven- to thirteen-year-olds are led by a couple of young teens, and the youngest group is led by some nine-year-olds, who take turns joining them. They play a game, look at a Bible story, sing some songs, and pray. The kids love it (as do the parents!), and you can tell that the children are tangibly growing in their walk with Jesus. A third children's small group is about to launch, as the overall community is growing quickly and the kids' small groups are proving to be a fruitful avenue.

What a wonderful picture of disciples making disciples! It's something so easy, "even" a child can do it!

WHAT IS A DISCIPLE?

When you look at Jesus and see the kind of person he is, the quality of life he lives, and the depth of character he has, do you ever wish that you could be more like him? We certainly do!

We have good news for you. If you share this desire to trust and imitate Jesus more closely and you are willing to commit to doing what it takes to look and live like him more consistently, then—bingo!—you are now a disciple of Jesus! Being a disciple of Jesus simply means that you are modeling your life—your thoughts, your words, your actions, your everything—after the example and teaching Jesus has given us. And the related word *discipleship* simply refers to the process through which Jesus turns us into people who trust and follow him.

A friend of ours put it like this:

A disciple is the kind of person who becomes the kind of person Jesus would be.

We love that! Wouldn't you like to be the kind of person who shows others what Jesus is like?

Bobby uses the following definition of a disciple:[1]

A disciple is someone who is following Jesus, being changed by Jesus, and is committed to Jesus' kingdom mission.

People like this definition because it ties together the focus (Jesus), the process (being changed), and the call to lead others to become disciples with us (Jesus' kingdom mission).

What we want you to see is that being a disciple is all about becoming like Jesus, and then helping others become like Jesus, because that is the way God has designed for us to experience fullness of life. One of our favorite verses in the Bible is John 10:10, where Jesus says, "I have come

that they may have life, and have it to the full." Becoming like Jesus is the
greatest thing we could ever wish for someone!

Alex uses a slightly different formulation of *disciple*, yet with the same
goal in mind:

A disciple is an intentional learner from Jesus.

Thus the two questions of discipleship are:

1. What is Jesus saying?
2. What am I doing in response?

As you will see in a moment, this definition picks up on the idea
that being a disciple is akin to being an apprentice, and that discipleship
is a dynamic process. The two questions—"What is Jesus saying?" and
"What am I doing in response?"—are like viruses when released into a
community! Whatever situation in life we are facing, we can use the two
questions of discipleship to stop and analyze the issue and then take the
next steps as followers of Jesus.

It's not hard to find lots of fabulous pithy statements that summarize
what it means to be a disciple. And
all of the best ones revolve around the
truth that a disciple hears and obeys
Jesus, leading to a lifestyle that reflects him well to the watching world.

A disciple hears and obeys Jesus, leading to a lifestyle that reflects him well to the watching world.

Since this book is all about discipleship and being a disciple of Jesus,
we think it is enormously helpful to begin here—with a simple phrase
that summarizes what being a disciple means in the context of your
local church. Such a description gives us something to aim at and neatly
provides us with a snapshot of what the church, as a Jesus-centered community, is all about. At a personal level, a definition of discipleship will
help you to make intentional choices in your everyday life that draw you
closer to Christlikeness.

Even though we don't all use exactly the same definition, it is essential
in every local church context to have a clear and Bible-based definition
so that people understand the goal—being disciples of Jesus. Of course,

there is value in going deeper, in tackling a far more detailed unpacking of what it means to be a disciple. Throughout the two-thousand-year history of the church, this journey of discipleship has been front and center in the thoughts and hearts of so many of the great men and women of God who have gone before us. Countless areas could be touched upon, and many excellent resources are available to help in areas where you are being challenged by Jesus to go deeper.

> **It is a myth that you can be discipled solely in one size of gathering.**

Such in-depth analysis of the content of discipleship is beyond the scope of this book. However, what this book will focus on is something that tends to get neglected in all the discussion about discipleship. We have found that having a clear definition of the goal is invaluable, *but equally important is understanding the different ways in which God works to shape us into disciples.* That's what this book is for. It is written to help you think about the different contexts in which Jesus disciples us.

You see, it is a myth that you can be discipled solely in one size of gathering, and we will show you how to set smart expectations for the different times and places where Jesus helps people to grow and mature. Before we jump into that, we need to add a few more brushstrokes to our understanding of how discipleship works.

WHAT IS DISCIPLESHIP?

We want to keep the concept of discipleship simple, and so we have a simple definition of it.[2] And though there are different terms for discipleship, each with its own nuance (which is very helpful), for the purposes of this book, we are going to equate the term *discipleship* with *disciple making.* So don't try to read any nuance into the words we use: discipleship means disciple making, and disciple making means discipleship.

Matthew 28:19–20 gives us a summary description of Jesus' discipleship mandate: "Therefore go and make disciples of all nations, baptizing them in the name of the Father and of the Son and of the Holy Spirit, and teaching them to obey everything I have commanded you. And surely I am with you always, to the very end of the age."

We do not use the exact words from this text, but we use the concepts and principles in a way that makes it easily applicable and repeatable today.[3] We simply tell people that disciple making is *helping people trust and follow Jesus*. The four concepts behind these verses provide us with four summary words: Help, Trust, Follow, and Jesus.

- *Help*: We are to initiate and be intentional—to "go" and "make disciples" (v. 19). We use the word *help* because it is a love-based word that sums up all the various intentional actions in disciple making, from *going* to *modeling* to *teaching* to *coaching* to *releasing*.
- *Trust*: Disciple making is about the heart change toward God upon which conversion/baptism is based—"baptizing them in the name of the Father and of the Son and of the Holy Spirit" (v. 19).
- *Follow*: Disciple making is about obedience and sanctification (increasing holiness)—"teaching them to obey everything I have commanded you" (v. 20).
- *Jesus*: He is both the focus and the constant presence in discipleship, just as he promised—"Surely I am with you always" (v. 20).

With these four components from Matthew 28 in mind, we define discipleship this way:

Discipleship is helping people to trust and follow Jesus.

As we said earlier, this is a simple definition, but don't assume it is simplistic. While it is easy to use and apply, it is comprehensive as well. Bobby uses this definition widely in the ministry of his church and discipleship.org, and he also has coauthored a book called *The Disciple Makers Handbook*, which describes in greater detail how everyday Christians live out this definition.[4]

We have found this definition to be easy to use in a local church context. High school students easily adopt it and grasp the key ideas. It is also easy to use in family life, where parents can use it with their children to help them grow into adulthood as people who trust and follow Jesus on their own.[5]

Trust and *follow* Jesus. *Trust* covers all the teachings in the Bible that call us to rely on God's grace, promises, and power. *Follow* encompasses all the teachings in the Bible that require us to respond to God—in obedience, faithfulness, and resistance to sin.

Both parts together capture the New Testament meaning of the word *faith*.[6] And both parts are consistent with the response necessitated by Jesus and his gospel.[7]

A Disciple Is an Apprentice

In the New Testament, the word for "disciple" (*mathetes*) occurs 264 times. In its original ancient Greek context, it meant someone who was either an apprentice in a trade or a pupil of a teacher.

Apprenticeship is a helpful picture for Jesus followers because it conveys the sense of a journey that cannot be bypassed in order to mature as a disciple. It takes time and practice to become a mature disciple, yet the only way you truly grow is by actually trying out the lifestyle you are observing. Apprenticeship allows us to gain a wonderful mix of both experience and knowledge, conveyed to us in the context of a long-term, deeply committed relationship. The Greek philosopher Aristotle noted that we owe more to our teachers than to our parents, since (as he put it) our parents give us life only, but our teachers give us the art of living well.

You see, the critical question that the ancients understood is this: "From whom are you learning?"

Put another way, a disciple is someone who is learning from a master craftsman.

For instance, if you want to learn how to do carpentry, you would be very unwise to ask me! I might be able to talk a good game for a minute or two, but you'd quickly realize I was scraping the barrel for information. A quick look in my garage would reveal that my carpentry tools are limited to a hammer (good for most things I find I need to do!) and a couple of quietly rusting saws tucked away in the corner. However, if I introduce you to my friend Dave, you would have an entirely different experience of carpentry. Dave is a master craftsman, with decades of experience in everything to do with woodwork. He has a truck full of all sorts of interesting-looking tools, many with the added bonus of power cords. Dave knows exactly what to do in every carpentry situation. He demonstrated that know-how to my family when he oversaw the task of finishing our basement, installing all sorts of items and hand building a perfect cupboard and shelving system that is the focal point of the room. If it had been left to me, there would be a couple of wobbly shelves clinging to the wall for dear life! When it comes to developing carpentry skills, you'd do well to learn from someone like my friend Dave.

When it comes to growing spiritually, from whom are you learning? And if your answer truly is Jesus, then what are you doing about what he is showing you?

To put that more precisely, what has Jesus been speaking to you about in the past seven days?

And what are you actually doing in response?

If you can't answer these questions, it's worth asking: Are you really committed to being an apprentice of Jesus?

Dallas Willard comments, "The assumption of Jesus' program for his people on earth was that they would live their lives as his students and co-laborers. They would find him so admirable in every respect—wise, beautiful, powerful, and good—that they would constantly seek to be in his presence and be guided, instructed, and helped by him in every aspect of their lives."[8]

Being a disciple means that I model my life around that of my master. I take note of how he lives, what he says, how he says it. I tease out his motivations and values so that when I encounter new situations, I can attempt to represent him faithfully. After each new experience, I discuss with him what went on and listen to his feedback, on both what went well and what could be improved next time. And then I try it out again.

Discipleship requires a humility that recognizes that I still have much to learn, and that because I belong to Jesus, he can send me into new places and situations. John Wimber describes this mindset: "A disciple is always ready to take the next step. If there is anything that characterizes Christian maturity, it is the willingness to become a beginner again for Jesus Christ. It is the willingness to put our hand in his and say, 'I'm scared to death, but I'll go with you. You're the Pearl of great price.'"[9]

As I do this, I learn to imitate what Jesus would do in the different situations and relationships of life.

Discipleship as Imitation

Because I (Alex) was raised in England, drinking tea is a central part of my cultural identity! Whatever the situation—a celebration, a welcome, a crisis, an afternoon break—the response of a good Brit is to put the kettle on and brew a pot of tea for everyone in the room to share.

Coming to the United States was quite a shock, mainly because everyone drank coffee and seemed ignorant of the vital role of tea in extending the kingdom of God. I would try explaining to my new colleagues that coffee is the devil's brew, and that the word *theist* means (1) someone who believes in a personal God and (2) someone who loves tea, ergo tea drinking is from Jesus, but my words had little impact.

I was greatly disheartened.

So I took a new approach. I brought an electric kettle and some tea into the office and simply made my own cup of tea. One of my colleagues was standing nearby and asked what I was doing. When I explained that I was making a cup of tea, she replied, "That looks nice—could you make me one?" As I did, I showed her the importance of boiling the water and allowing the tea to brew and explained why milk works better than cream. So she went off to her desk with her cup of tea and no doubt produced some of the finest work of her career over the rest of the morning. The next day she saw me and declared that she'd really enjoyed her tea, and could I show her again how I made it just right, which of course I gladly did.

> In order to bear fruit as we follow Jesus, we need to grasp the centrality of discipleship as imitation.

A couple of days later I was walking down the corridor and passed one of my other colleagues, who was carrying what looked like a cup of tea. "That looks nice—do you drink tea?"

"Not until yesterday, but I saw Su drinking tea, so I asked her to make me a cup as well. You should try it sometime!"

Over the next few months the number of tea drinkers slowly went up, the supplies of tea in the staff room increased, and the coffeepot looked lonelier and lonelier. Tea drinking had become the dominant source of refreshment, and the shift had come about through a process of discipleship by imitation.

So often we in the church focus the vast bulk of our discipling (and evangelistic) energies on the transfer of information. And while there certainly is an unending depth to what we believe, an overemphasis on information transfer is not the most effective way to disciple others—and definitely is not the predominant biblical pattern.

In order to bear fruit as we follow Jesus, we need to grasp the centrality of discipleship as imitation.

Paul on Discipleship as Imitation

As you read the New Testament, you might be surprised to know that Paul's emphasis is not on convincing us to accept abstract propositional truths. After all, some of those harder-to-understand sections of his letters seem at first glance to be all about that!

Yet if we truly look at what Paul teaches, reading his words in parallel with the accounts of his ministry in the book of Acts, a different picture emerges. While he teaches us fundamental doctrine, shares wonderful insights, and loves to demonstrate the intellectual rigor behind submitting to Jesus, his repeated focus is on living out what we know about God in the world around us. He himself was an apprentice in multiple areas (in the world of tent making, as a Pharisee under Gamaliel, and then notably to Barnabas) and in turn apprenticed many men and women in how to live a life worthy of the Lord (as he prayed in Col. 1:10). Paul understood that for most people, faith in Jesus is best transferred and deepened in the context of relational experiences.

Thus Paul wrote to the Christians in Corinth, "Follow my example, as I follow the example of Christ" (1 Cor. 11:1), and "Therefore I urge you to imitate me" (1 Cor. 4:16). That's bold stuff! But it wasn't a one-off challenge for a unique situation.

To the church in Philippi he instructed, "Join together in following my example, brothers and sisters, and just as you have us as a model, keep your eyes on those who live as we do" (Phil. 3:17). In the following chapter, Paul added, "Whatever you have learned or received or heard from me, or seen in me—put it into practice" (Phil. 4:9).

The same understanding of discipleship as imitation was taught to the Thessalonian Christians. "You became imitators of us and of the Lord"

(1 Thess. 1:6), followed up with this reminder in 2 Thessalonians 3:7: "You yourselves know how you ought to follow our example." As an aside, personally I find that these verses doubly challenge me: Am I following the example of Christ in other believers, and is my example worth others following?

Paul spent a number of years living in the city of Ephesus and knew that church very well. Therefore we should not be surprised when we read, "Follow God's example, therefore, as dearly loved children and walk in the way of love" (Eph. 5:1–2). For Paul, the journey of discipleship was founded upon a lifestyle of imitation—direct imitation of Jesus as well as imitation of the lives of other believers around us, especially those we are learning from and following.

PLAY WHILE BEING COACHED

The New Testament model of disciple making is essentially to call people to play their part in the church from day one—to jump into the game—and for that to be the context for their discipleship. We are encouraged to try out what we believe, and to be apprenticed as we do so.

Where it raises anxiety about the risk of error in belief or practice, this apprenticeship approach is far from allowing an "anything goes" mindset. We must receive robust coaching as we grow (from the Holy Spirit, the Bible, and other believers), which is one of the reasons Paul places such a strong emphasis on tying discipleship to the local church. You cannot have a culture of empowerment without a parallel value of accountability.

You cannot have a culture of empowerment without a parallel value of accountability.

Which, of course, is how we best train people in any area of life.

I (Alex) have three teenage sons, who either have gone or will go through the nerve-shredding rite of learning to drive a car. While they have to study the driver's manual (or *The Digest of Ohio Motor Vehicle Laws*, as one state snappily titles it) and go to classes, ultimately they won't learn to drive by reading a book or hearing a lecture, but by sitting behind the wheel and scaring the whatnots out of their long-suffering parents. After yet another near-miss I'll sit there thinking, "I'm paying for this. I must be mad." But it is the only way for them to grow into safe and responsible drivers, who one day will be so good at driving that they will pass on their skills to their children.

Apprenticeship really does work. But we need to understand the way in which it operates.

The way Jesus does apprenticeship is through three broad elements: relationships, experiences, and information.

REI—RELATIONSHIPS, EXPERIENCES, AND INFORMATION

> *Tell me and I'll forget; show me and I may remember;*
> *involve me and I'll understand.*
> —*Chinese proverb*

We're going to give you a quick game to play, but you'll need a scrap of paper to do so.

First off, set a timer for one minute. Now press "Start" and write down the five sermons you have heard that have most drawn you closer to Jesus.

No overrunning on time!

Now reset the timer, and in one minute record the five experiences that have most drawn you closer to Jesus.

Finally, take one minute to name the five people who have most drawn you closer to Jesus.

Look at the three lists and answer these questions: Which one was easiest to write? And which one was toughest to complete?

If you are like the hundreds of people we have tested this on, you found it hardest to think of the five sermons (we're church pastors, and we struggle to list five life-changing sermons that we've heard ourselves preach!). The experiences will be easier to come up with, but the clear winner is almost always the relationships. We bet you could comfortably list more than five names in one minute.

What this game illustrates is that God has wired us to be highly relational beings. While all sorts of things can shape us, the deepest impact on our core being comes from the investment of others in our lives. They may be coaching us in a specific skill, but their character, love, and lifestyle will go deeper and farther into our lives.

Discipleship is primarily about imitation over information, and it is through relationships that it most powerfully occurs. Now to be clear, viewing discipleship this way is not an anti-intellectual approach—together we have spent thirteen years studying theology full-time, and we remain very grateful for that opportunity and those who taught us—but it is about resetting our perspective. Most of us have been raised in the Western world that has been heavily influenced by Enlightenment thinking, which prioritizes the mind and our rationality over everything else. Unfortunately, just thinking clever thoughts does not produce disciples who are ready to go and make other disciples.

Good discipleship is a balance of relationships, experiences, and information. Regrettably, the Western church has the tendency to emphasize information downloading over relational discipleship. Instead, relationships should be the highest priority, the context in which we disciple others life on life, combining love and invitation with vision and challenge. And experiences play their part, as through them—whether it's as simple as sharing a meal together, serving alongside someone, or going away on a trip or retreat—we have an external context for the working out of an internal transformation.

The information element is also far richer within the framework of relationships, as questions are asked, dialogue takes place, specific applications are made, and together we learn what it means to know and follow God. Done in this order, we make dynamic disciples of Jesus; done in reverse, we make Pharisees.

Let's consider how we see Jesus making disciples in the Gospels.

JESUS ON DISCIPLESHIP

In Matthew 11 Jesus invites us to come to him if we are weary, to give him our burdens, and in exchange to receive his rest. To drive home the point, in verses 29–30 he uses the following farming illustration: "Take my yoke upon you and learn from me, for I am gentle and humble in heart, and you will find rest for your souls. For my yoke is easy and my burden is light."

A yoke is a large piece of timber that is carved and shaped to sit comfortably on the shoulders of a specific ox, and then extends across to a second creature, which also receives that custom molding of the wood. If the fit is not done well, the animal will end up with sores on its shoulders and be unable to plow effectively, if at all.

If you put yourself in the hooves of an ox, you'll find it is not the most natural thing to be hitched alongside another ox and forced to walk in straight lines across a field all day long. To counter this, the way farmers train a younger animal is to pair it up with an older ox, who can model how to recognize and respond to the farmer's commands, to plow in the direction he needs you to go, and to carry the yoke in a way that is comfortable and sustainable.

Here Jesus is using the picture of carrying his yoke to illustrate how he disciples us.

For spiritual people at the time of Jesus, the yoke represented something negative: obligation and oppression, keeping the law as interpreted by the Jewish traditions, trying to earn your way closer to God. It was an uncomfortable constraint that people had to bear in order to try to move in God's direction.

But Jesus completely turned that around. What he places upon us is something perfectly formfitting, designed to steer us in the right direction at his lightest touch, so that we can truly honor God and live in such a way that we bring him a great return.

His invitation is into an apprenticeship, to become a disciple who learns from a gentle, kind, and loving Master who doesn't have an unhealthy ego that must be maneuvered around first. Jesus is enormously attractive in his personality, and we are rightly drawn to know him better and become more like him in our own characters. John Ortberg says, "This is why Jesus came. This is what spiritual life is about. This is your calling—to become what [C. S.] Lewis calls an 'everlasting splendor.'"[10] To be a disciple is to become increasingly like Jesus in our character as we reflect the attractiveness of his personality.

As we choose the path of discipleship, an inexpressible peace and rest will fall upon our souls. Of course, if we think of this rest as equating to lots of time lying on the beach, then we miss the point of what Jesus is saying here: discipleship is a lifestyle far more than it is an event, and it is a posture from which we can engage with the world in a healthy and fruitful way.

When Jesus invites us to accept his yoke, we can be confident that it will train and mature us to make an impact for him. In addition, we are reminded that we don't do discipleship flying solo—we will always be connected to other people so that we can both imitate and be imitated as we go through life, pointing people to maturity in Christ.

FINDING THE ANCIENT PATHS

In speaking of rest for our souls, Jesus also may have been thinking of the prophecy in Jeremiah 6:16:

> "Stand at the crossroads and look;
>   ask for the ancient paths,
> ask where the good way is, and walk in it,
>   and you will find rest for your souls."

God makes the first move in reaching out to us with an invitation to follow him. As we begin to walk in the pathways of the kingdom of God, even if much still needs sorting out within our hearts, we experience his grace and thus come to an increased understanding of his truth. As we choose to imitate Jesus, we enter into his eternal rest here on earth today.

In an intriguing statement, Jesus put it like this in John 8:31–32: "If you hold to my teaching, you are really my disciples. Then you will know the truth, and the truth will set you free."

The order here seems opposite of what we would expect: Jesus wants us to start doing what he does and saying what he says—holding to his teaching—and only then will the truth come and set us free.

Some churches (and church leaders) do this the opposite way. They say: "If you believe what we believe (because what we say is the fullest expression of God's truth, especially compared to that church/pastor down the road), and do/sign the thing we make people do/sign to demonstrate that they believe what we say, *then* we will start to disciple and invest in you. And if you don't rock the boat, we'll let you help us do what Jesus told you to do."

All of which is, of course, a complete reversal both of what Jesus said to do and of what Jesus actually did.

Jesus discipled those around him into the knowledge of the truth while being fully aware that some might not come to accept and believe that truth. He was willing to take that risk—and, as the Gospels make clear, people did walk away from him as they encountered his truth. So either Jesus was a terrible discipler of people, or he really meant it when he said we need to be discipled into all truth, rather than first having to accept the truth before we can be discipled!

Again, we believe that the truth that Jesus brings is absolutely vital, but he knows how we will best be transformed by it—by walking the path of a disciple. In other words, discipleship takes time and is built on relationships and experiences, which provide a context for information to be internalized. And our primary relationship is with Jesus himself and consists of the experiences we have with him.

GOD DISCIPLES PEOPLE THROUGH RELATIONSHIP

We've just provided a very brief introduction to the concept of discipleship and the importance of relationships in the process. If we were to summarize the key points in this book, we'd say it this way:

1. God disciples us.
2. God disciples us *through relationships*.
3. God disciples us through relationships *differently in different relational contexts*.

The Great Commission in Matthew 28 assumes two very important things that we want to note: God has commanded that we *make disciples*, and Jesus is *with us* in the process, working through us. Our part is to

Our part is to make disciples and Jesus' promise is to be with us as he makes disciples through us.

make disciples and Jesus' promise is to be with us as he makes disciples through us.

In a slightly different context, Richard Foster, in his book *Celebration of Discipline*, gives us a helpful metaphor for God's role and our role in disciple making. He gets us to "picture a long, narrow ridge with a sheer drop-off on either side."[11] The chasm to the right is the way of strictly human effort. It is where we try to make disciples in our own strength and power, through our goals, plans, and schemes alone. This approach is based on a misguided focus on and trust in ourselves. But the chasm to the left can be just as dangerous; in the absence of human effort and participation, we just leave it all up to God, taking no responsibility for ourselves or those around us.

On the ridge between the two extremes is a path. It is the path where God is at work in us as we make disciples. It is God's Spirit, God's power, and God's presence, moving through our efforts (as disciples and disciple makers), that molds people increasingly into the image of Jesus (2 Cor. 3:17–18). The apostle Paul astutely sums up our role and God's role in 2 Corinthians 3:2–3: "You yourselves are our letter, written on our hearts, known and read by everyone. You show that you are a letter from Christ, the result of our ministry, written not with ink but with the Spirit of the living God, not on tablets of stone but on tablets of human hearts."

While we could write an entire book on avoiding these two extremes, that's not our focus here. We want to emphasize that there are specific and contextual ways in which God disciples us, namely through other people.

And that brings us back to the main topic of this book: God uses people to disciple us differently in different relational contexts. We see this through the ways Jesus did his own discipleship. There were times when Jesus impacted people through a sermon delivered to hundreds, other occasions when he was shaping a midsized community in the thirties or forties in number, and other times when he was discipling just his small group of twelve. And then again, sometimes Peter, James, and John were the only ones Jesus was discipling. Added to these four contexts, of course, are the times when Jesus directly discipled without the involvement of others.

We believe you will be much more effective in helping people trust and follow Jesus if you understand what God *typically* does in each of these "five contexts" of discipleship. Knowledge is power, because knowing what is most effective in a particular context empowers you to make the biggest difference.

DISCIPLESHIP MATTERS

Discipleship matters because it is at the center of what Jesus has commissioned his followers to be about. Not only does discipleship summarize God's interactions with us, but it should be the primary way we invest ourselves in others.

Yet to be effective disciple makers, most of us will need to go through a "debugging," dismantling the false understandings we have of what it means to be a disciple of Jesus. That's why in our next chapter we are going to spend some time reimagining discipleship for the post-Christian culture in which most of us find ourselves living. Then in the following chapter we'll give you an overview of the core content of this book—the Five Contexts of Discipleship.

After that will flow five pairs of chapters, each looking at one of the Five Contexts, to give both an understanding of how each operates and examples of how certain aspects of discipleship come to the fore in specific sizes of gatherings. By becoming aware of the strengths and weaknesses of each of the Five Contexts, you will be better equipped to set realistic expectations as well as navigate around common frustrations.

Finally, we want to mention that this book has been coauthored. Alex wrote chapters 2 through 7, as well as chapter 14, and Bobby penned chapters 8 through 13. But we didn't write alone. We helped each other on our respective chapters so the entire book speaks with one voice. The way we split the writing of the chapters reflects our own particular areas of expertise, practice, and study. We hope you will be challenged (as we have been) as you read through your own areas of inexperience, as well as those where you are stronger.

Chapter Two

YOU'RE NOT CRAMMING
FOR AN EXAM

Discipleship, Evangelism,
and the Cross

If you visit the headquarters of the Central Intelligence Agency of the US government, you will see the words "And Ye Shall Know the Truth and the Truth Shall Make You Free" inscribed on the floor of the entrance concourse. Taken from the passage we looked at earlier in John 8, these words embrace a worthy desire to know truth and to bring freedom—but they miss the critical step. The journey toward truth starts with becoming a follower of *Jesus*. He is the Truth.

We misunderstand discipleship if we focus on the forensic pursuit of truth in such a way that we forget that it is all about a friendship with Jesus. Being a friend of God is the basis for understanding the secrets of the kingdom of God (see Matt. 13:11). As Dallas Willard comments, "If I am Jesus' disciple that means I am with him to learn from him how to be like him."[12]

Have you ever noticed how so many of the great heroes of the Bible—those from whom we learn so much about being a disciple—are described in language that talks of their being friends of God?

We think of God choosing to bring Abraham into the conversation about the judgment of Sodom and Gomorrah in Genesis 18:17–19, or the summary verse about Moses in Exodus 33:11, "The LORD would speak to Moses face to face, as one speaks to a friend." Hebrews 11 famously lists many of the great men and women of faith in the Old Testament, and it is clear that their commendation is related to their friendship level of trust in God. He was no remote deity to these people: he was, to quote Solomon, that "friend who sticks closer than a brother" (Prov. 18:24). As that Hall of Fame chapter comments, "Therefore God is not ashamed to be called their God, for he has prepared a city for them" (Heb. 11:16).

The greatest illustration of this connection between discipleship and friendship comes from the lips of Jesus in the hours before the crucifixion: "I no longer call you servants, because a servant does not know his master's business. Instead, I have called you friends, for everything that I learned from my Father I have made known to you" (John 15:15).

These examples are no accident—because discipleship and true friendship are closely aligned.

The way we enter into a friendship with God is entirely at his initiative. None of us have any right to demand anything from him, and we certainly don't have the power to force anything on him!

Yet because of his intrinsic relational wiring, God has reached out to us in Jesus, inviting us into relationship with him, dealing decisively with what damages our relationship, namely our sin. At the cross, Jesus died in our place not only so we can experience forgiveness of sin, but also so we can live a life of purpose and significance today—as God's apprentices.

What finer destiny could there be than becoming more Christlike in nature and lifestyle, bound ever more closely to God in love and friendship, representing him wherever we go through our words and works? Such is the wonder of discipleship!

UNDER GOD'S STEAM

The lack of discipleship undermines all else that we seek to do.
—Alan Hirsch

If you are like me (Alex) in desiring to represent Jesus anywhere and everywhere, then you also realize that you simply don't have the capacity to pull that off consistently and convincingly under your own steam. Speaking personally, even as someone who daily receives afresh the forgiveness and new life of Jesus, I still mess up and know that I can't really represent God with much effectiveness just by trying harder. I need help. (No doubt many people have thought that about me, even if they've been kind enough not to blurt it out to my face!)

The Holy Spirit has many roles, but one of them is to come along-side us as disciples of Jesus and empower us to live differently. As Jesus reminded the first disciples, "You will receive power when the Holy Spirit comes on you; and you will be my witnesses . . ." (Acts 1:8).

Wherever you are in your walk with God, God's Spirit stands ready and able to help, to guide, to give you wisdom and strength so that you genuinely start to change and live differently. Whether you are thinking about relationships, experiences, or information, the Holy Spirit can and will help you.

> **The Holy Spirit has many roles, but one of them is to come alongside us as disciples of Jesus and empower us to live differently.**

The work of the Holy Spirit in our lives is far-reaching and so very needed. But we must realize that our relationship with him is a part-nership and that we must play our part as well. Sometimes learning and growing as a disciple is fun and rewarding, but other times it can be challenging and costly.

THE COST OF DISCIPLESHIP

> *If anyone would come after me, let him deny himself*
> *and take up his cross daily and follow me.*
> —*Luke 9:23 ESV*

> *When Christ calls a man, he bids him come and die.*
> —*Dietrich Bonhoeffer, The Cost of Discipleship*

Our Western world highly values comfort and ease. Those are not bad things—for instance, I love all the electronic gizmos that are so fun to play with! However, the temptation is to take from supplementary blessings a principle that becomes primary.

In the context of discipleship, then, we need to understand that discipleship is *not* about our comfort. It is not all sunshine, prizes, and fragrant flowers with unicorns sitting on top! And here's why:

God is most interested not in making us happy but in making us holy.

In the Bible, the word *holy* is never fully defined. That's because it is a way of summarizing the very nature of God—God is holy, and thus to be holy is to be like God. "Be holy, because I am holy" (Lev. 11:44).

Of course, God is a generous and loving Father who is thrilled at any opportunity to pour out tangible blessings into our lives. But at the same time he is not misty-eyed about the big picture; that is, he is working to make us mature in Christ and to see more of his kingdom revealed in this broken world. And this means that, while salvation is free, discipleship comes at a cost.

David Watson commented, "Every Christian is called to a clear and dedicated discipleship, whatever the personal cost may be."[13] Jesus talked about this in Luke 14:26–27: "If anyone comes to me and does not hate father and mother, wife and children, brothers and sisters—yes, even their own life—such a person cannot be my disciple. And whoever does not carry their cross and follow me cannot be my disciple."

Consider the paradoxical nature of discipleship:

- A disciple receives friendship with Jesus as a gift—but then must lay everything down to follow through on that relational commitment.

- A disciple sees Jesus as better than life itself—but life itself is enriched to the max when we follow Jesus.

- A disciple prioritizes Jesus over every other relationship— but every other relationship is made richer in Jesus.

This sounds like a tall order—and, of course, it is. But since discipleship is imitation, we are not left alone to work out how to do these things. Jesus went ahead of us when he counted the cost, gave up far more than any of us will have to sacrifice, and chose to take the path to the cross, both literally and figuratively. And he tells us, "Those of you who do not give up everything you have cannot be my disciples" (Luke 14:33).

> A disciple prioritizes Jesus over every other relationship— but every other relationship is made richer in Jesus.

Being a disciple of Jesus is not easy. Sometimes we may feel like we're being challenged beyond the breaking point—and we're tempted to wonder if the sacrifices we've made are worth it. But then we bring to mind the big picture of what the Lord is doing in our lives, of the way he is moving through us in the lives of others, of how our church community is representing him in our place of mission. And while being a disciple still can be enormously challenging, we know that we are sacrificing for the greatest of causes.

A wise disciple counts the cost and is willing to pay the price.

GO AND MAKE DISCIPLES

> *Ultimately, each church will be evaluated*
> *by only one thing—its disciples.*
> —*Neil Cole, Ordinary Hero*

If you are a follower of Jesus, you have been commissioned by him to go and make disciples. In Matthew 28:19–20 he summarizes the call in these famous words: "Therefore go and make disciples of all nations, baptizing them in the name of the Father and of the Son and of the Holy Spirit, and teaching them to obey everything I have commanded you." As an expression of your love for God and neighbor, there is no more meaningful task to which you can give yourself.

Yet too often we have a faulty understanding of what it means to go and make disciples—because we do not in our hearts have real faith that Jesus' discipleship model actually works. We think of discipleship as the transfer of knowledge, and if we're really spiritual we do some good deeds. But really discipleship is about a change of heart. The doing comes out of a new heart (and only then does it not burn you out or turn into legalism).

Our friend Jim Putnam tells the story of when he realized he didn't actually know how to make disciples. What he'd been taught was how to teach a class, prepare a sermon, and make a pastoral call. As Jesus was challenging him about this, and about the lack of fruit being produced, he reflected on the place in his life where he had most experienced discipleship—through the sport of wrestling. Jim took on the lifestyle of his wrestling coach in an effort to immerse himself in the sport and thus become very good at it. As he looked at the principles of how he'd been trained, he was able to translate them to Christian discipleship.

This experience played out further in his life when he felt called to plant a new church. Feeling pressured to put on a big show, he realized that he and his team just didn't have the resources to do that. So they decided that their most important thing would not be the church service. Instead, they recognized that people needed relationship and answers for life, and that's what they would offer.

Jim notes that we tend to concentrate on the masses instead of the few because we think that's quicker. Yet Jesus interacted with thousands but focused on a few in order to reach the thousands.[14]

In case those of you with existing churches are worried, we are not going to argue that you should scrap your weekend worship service! Far from it. As the chapters on the Public Context will demonstrate, we strongly believe church services have enormous value. The hazard that must be avoided, however, is expecting that this larger gathering will somehow magically do things that it simply is not set up to do very well.

However, what we are saying is that in all five of the contexts of discipleship, the essence of our transformation is always our relationship with God, lived out through relationship with others. This means that if you are not in relationship with God and in relationship with others, loving them well, you are not making disciples.

Discipleship is always relational. Don't just take our word for it though. Have you ever noticed how each of the fruits of the Spirit is relational? That's because discipleship is always relational! In a world of loneliness, people know they need the love that ultimately comes from God, enfleshed in those around them who follow that same God.

Effective disciples of Jesus must have an unshakable conviction that relational discipleship is the smartest and most biblical way to reach the world. Unless you believe that at the core of your being, you will continually focus on being externally successful, striving after the things that bring acclaim or affirmation.

EVANGELISM, DISCIPLESHIP, AND THE CROSS

Throughout this book we will be arguing that God disciples us through five distinct contexts: the Public, the Social, the Personal, the Transparent, and the Divine. Undergirding this argument, however, is an assumption we have made about how evangelism and discipleship interrelate.

Traditionally, many Christians talk about evangelism—someone's response to the message of the gospel—as happening up to the point of conversion, when an individual consciously commits to Christ as Savior and Lord. After that, the focus of our efforts shifts to discipleship, as the new Christian learns how to follow through on that commitment within the context of the church. Such a process can be illustrated as in figure 1.

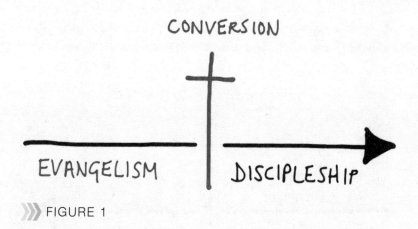

》》 FIGURE 1

We believe, however, that this traditional view is not a biblical pattern. Here's why.

Evangelism is clearly biblical. But it does not end at the point of conversion. As a follower of Jesus, I need to hear afresh the challenge and encouragement of the gospel and respond to it.[15] There will always be days when God calls me to repent of some instance when I failed to act with godly patience (not one of my most natural personality traits!). Ideally, over time, fewer areas of my life will be in open rebellion, but that doesn't mean I no longer need to hear the gospel. So the gospel is not just something we use in evangelism—it is a key aspect of our discipleship as well.

Hopefully most of you can agree with that. But we want to take this idea one step farther by flipping it around. When it comes to discipleship, our experience is that people far from God can be discipled where they are today. They might be light-years from acknowledging Christ as Savior and Lord, but they are open to learning from him (perhaps as he lives in you) in a certain area of life. For instance, I have found my neighbors to be very open to learning from Jesus about parenting, or caring for the vulnerable, or handling finances, and so on.

One way of describing this truth is to say that discipleship begins at "Hello."

Discipleship begins at "Hello."

Nowhere does the New Testament indicate that a person must attain a certain level of knowledge before they can officially commence the journey of discipleship.

To help illustrate, figure 2 shows a modified version of figure 1.

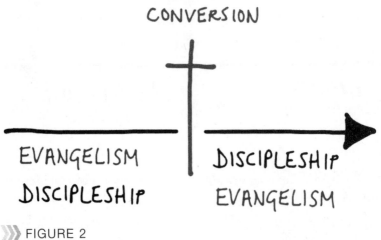

CONVERSION

EVANGELISM
DISCIPLESHIP

DISCIPLESHIP
EVANGELISM

》》 FIGURE 2

Here you can see that both evangelism (responding to the challenge of the gospel) and discipleship (hearing what Jesus is saying and then doing something about it) are ongoing works in our lives. While evangelism and discipleship are distinct areas, they are far more closely related than many realize, and they certainly don't operate in a linear manner ("I must complete the whole process—or event—of evangelism before I can begin discipleship"). As N. T. Wright has shown, the good news changes everything, every day.[16] Jesus and his resurrection bring an entirely new perspective to life. We believe he will come back soon and fully consummate and establish his kingdom. So on a daily basis we respond to the gospel and live as disciples of King Jesus. While there is a more obvious emphasis on evangelism in the early stages, it is ultimately unhelpful to separate evangelism from discipleship. They are organically entwined and feed off each other, working together in our walk with Jesus.

Bounded Set Discipleship

To underscore this understanding of discipleship as a journey that is open to all, some very helpful insights are available to us in the sociology of sets, which look at how groups of people connect over a period of time. Broadly speaking, there are three types of sets: bounded, fuzzy, and centered.[17]

The bounded set is, unsurprisingly, focused on the *boundary* that determines who is inside and who is outside a specific group. A classic example would be a country club, where those who pay the fees, keep the rules, and satisfy the requirements of the leadership committee are allowed to be members of the club. So if you roll up at the front gate on a hot summer's day with your swim gear, the only way you are using the pool is if you are a member. There are no exceptions! This is a binary world—either you are in or you are out.

In figure 3, the circle represents the boundary, and the arrows are different people. Many (arrow A) try to enter but fail to clear the fence around the organization and are turned away. A few (arrow B) manage to hop inside but become like arrow C—drifting around with no further meaningful goals or objectives. As long as they don't upset the leadership (represented by the crown, as they often have near absolute authority!), they can stay in the group.

The church often operates like a bounded set. We create our boundary—perhaps sitting through sixteen hours of membership classes, or being baptized, or speaking in tongues, or believing what we believe on end-times theology (because we are the ones who have finally decoded the mystery)—and then we devote an enormous amount of energy to enforcing that separation. This boundary, we imply, is the litmus test for a disciple.

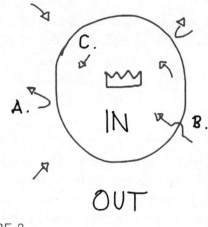

》 FIGURE 3

Of course none of those things listed as church boundaries are intrinsically wrong, but by overemphasizing a few specifics we raise the bar beyond what Jesus requires, keeping many from experiencing what it means to follow Jesus. Those who pass the test are now on the inside, but where are they going after they get in? Where is the ongoing sense of pilgrimage, of growth and maturation as a follower of Jesus Christ? Instead of seeing themselves as apprentices, people in churches like this take on an entitlement mentality. They are in the club, and membership has its privileges! Thus we build a culture that produces Christian consumers rather than Christian disciples, and then we wonder why we aren't growing missional leaders in the kingdom of God.

A bounded set mentality can also hinder our missional openness. Considerable research has been conducted on how group affiliation takes place, with fascinating results. In *The Respect Effect*, Paul Meshanko concludes, "We are much more likely to treat others in ways that communicate value if we perceive that they are, somehow, like us. . . . Controlled experiments consistently show that we are more courteous, generous, and empathetic towards those with whom we share some meaningful common bond."[18]

A church that is seeking to be missionally fruitful and to reach previously unreached people groups must be willing to build authentic Christian community with people *who are not like themselves.* This requires a different sociological underpinning for how we affiliate with others, particularly in our understanding of how the church is bound together.

Fuzzy Set Discipleship

In response to a bounded set style of discipleship, some brave souls may decide to break away from the institution. Declaring that all are welcome into their group, they say that since all are equal in God's sight there is no need for leaders or boundaries. After all, wasn't the New Testament church all about valuing and sharing the varied gifts of the body of Christ?

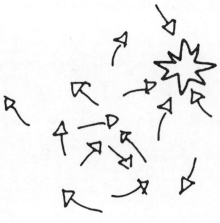

>>> FIGURE 4

This "fuzzy set" approach feels wonderful at first. Everything is so relaxed and relational, especially when compared to the more controlling bounded set environment. In figure 4, where the arrows represent people, everyone can move around as they please. It's something of a hippy paradise!

Unfortunately, this collegial climate doesn't last long. Without a defining identity or clear direction, conflicts inevitably emerge (represented in the figure by the starburst). A choice presents itself, a decision has to be made about which way to turn, but group consensus can't be reached. Two dominant individuals fall out, and no system is in place to deal with the collateral damage. People begin to pull away, and the group dissipates like a mist on a sunny day.

While fuzzy set discipleship sounds ideal in theory, in practice it simply is not robust enough to deal with the fallen nature of humanity.

Centered Set Discipleship

Our third option, then, is a centered set community. Here, the key element is a defining idea that exists at the center of the group's life, giving it cohesiveness, direction, and structure. This defining idea might be a particular service that is offered, an item that is manufactured, a charitable work that is undertaken, or something else.

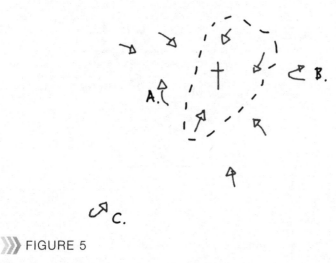

>>> FIGURE 5

For the disciple-making church, the uniting idea is actually a person, and his name is Jesus (represented in figure 5 by the cross at the center). We are together on a journey toward Christ and Christlikeness. None of us make it all the way there in this life, but with Jesus at the center, we have a vision to unite us and a framework for resolving every dilemma and relational difficulty (if we will hear and obey!). As a friend put it to me (Alex) recently, "The journey toward Christ is the primary point where doctrine and practice meet."

And here is where the type of "set" we adopt matters for discipleship. In its posture toward the world, a centered set church will invite even the most notorious of sinners to learn from Jesus, even

With Jesus at the center, we have a vision to unite us.

if most everything in their life bears little resemblance to him (arrow C in the figure). This open posture creates a low bar of entry yet does not require that we compromise the demands of the gospel. The point is less about getting someone over a somewhat arbitrary boundary and more about inviting everyone to take their next step toward Jesus. As Jim Putman writes, "Most of the time when discipleship is intentional, spiritual growth happens quickly."[19]

Of course, the centered set approach is not without difficulties. We need to take into account the context and the particular situation. So, for instance, churches do need leadership, and the dotted line represents the higher level of maturity that is expected of leaders (and clearly documented in the Scriptures). Where to place that line will vary between churches, and there should be some fluidity in how people can move in and out of a leadership role. (You are a leader only for as long as you are leading, not for as long as you hold a particular office!) Likewise, not all people will keep moving toward Jesus at the center. Some will go so far and then be comfortable going into orbit around Jesus (arrow A), while others will be offended by a fresh challenge and choose to turn away from Jesus, in at least one aspect of their life (arrow B).

Of course, Jesus speaks clearly in John 3 of the shift that occurs when we are born again, and he presents that shift as a radical change. Matthew 25 includes repeated challenges to make the right choice in the ultimate binary decision: wise or foolish virgin, faithful or unfaithful servant, sheep or goat.

Yet in each instance, the call is to commit to following Jesus, to trust in a Person, or as John comments, to "believe in him" (John 3:16). While doctrine is of vital importance, ultimately the call is to far more than simply holding the right set of theological propositions in your head. To truly follow Jesus as Lord is an all-encompassing commitment that transforms everything.

Along the way, Jesus is gracious enough to give us significant moments that we can memorialize to represent key steps in our journey. Thus I can recall the day I finally went all in with Jesus and sincerely prayed a prayer of surrender and commitment (August 25, 1984, if you are interested!). But that deeply significant moment was never intended to become a boundary from behind which I could divide the world in two, defining how I would interact with each person once I had correctly categorized them.

Indeed, if I find myself closer to Jesus than my neighbor, my job is to do all I can to live out how to move toward Jesus in tangible ways that make sense to them where they are today, in a relationship of grace, acceptance, and generosity. This doesn't mean I ignore sin and wrong belief, and certainly my life should look different, but it does mean that I don't spend my energy judging lost people by the values of the kingdom they have yet to embrace. As my friend Ben Sternke puts it, I must be both high connection and high distinction.

Churches will also need to consider how a centered set approach impacts the practice of church discipline. In a bounded set, it will be clear who is subject to discipline, but in a centered set there are some gray areas. For what it's worth, my (Alex's) personal view is that church discipline is effective only where there is already an existing relationship (otherwise, why would the person be governed or concerned by it?). Where relationship and accountability already exist, discipline actually fits well as part of the pilgrimage culture that is being developed. Bobby supports a covenant membership paradigm because of this point. In this concept, once a person has fully committed to trust and follow Jesus, they believe it is a good thing to choose to be in covenant with a local body of believers where accountability like that described in Matthew 18:15–17 is upheld. The concept of church discipline is complex, and not all will agree on its implementation. We both agree that there are times when we need to be challenged and held accountable, as that is part of what it means to grow in Christlikeness. We also agree it is a tricky principle to apply, requiring much prayer and guidance by the Holy Spirit. Different leaders will choose to handle discipline differently (at the membership and leadership levels). Yet the dotted line indicates that discipline remains part of a centered set, where people are working out their beliefs, relationships, and behavior in the context of journey.

In summary, when these sociological understandings are coupled with a biblical understanding of how evangelism and discipleship work simultaneously in our lives, we have a strong framework for shaping a disciple-making culture within a local church.

GOD USES EVERY SITUATION

Thus far we have defined discipleship. We have addressed the need for relationships. And we've seen how the sociological context can affect the way we engage in discipleship. But let's broaden our perspective further by looking at the when and where of discipleship. We want to suggest that God can—and does—disciple us in *every* situation of life, in *every* type of relational interaction, and that he uses *different* situations and relationships in *different* ways.

> God can—and does—disciple us in *every* situation of life, in *every* type of relational interaction.

We are continually engaging with people in various situations and in various sizes of gatherings. I see this in my own life when I'm with hundreds, perhaps walking around the grocery store, watching a football game, singing in a Sunday morning worship service, or typing my status into Facebook or Twitter.

Other times I'm with dozens of other people, for instance, gathering with the neighbors for a grill-out, joining in a family reunion, or sharing in a missional community.

I also have interactions with just a handful of people, whether debating with colleagues in a meeting at work, playing soccer with the guys on my team, engaging the members of a small group, or enjoying those who will sit around the dining room table with me for dinner this evening.

Then there are the deepest relationships, where I'm sharing the latest installment of life's story with my closest friends and family, perhaps giving focused attention to one of my children, talking on the phone to my best man, or, most clearly, spending time one-on-one with my wife!

Finally come those times when I'm alone, maybe watching a TV show, singing in the shower, reading my Bible and praying, or driving to work and thinking about an upcoming appointment.

Jesus will disciple us in each of these five sizes of gatherings—if we will let him. Our task is to invite him to do so, to look for opportunities to be discipled, and to set the right expectations for the outcomes of each of those different contexts. As we embrace these varied places and times of discipleship, simultaneously our eyes will be opened to see the opportunities that exist to disciple others.

In the next chapter we will give you an overview of how the Five Contexts of discipleship work, along with an introduction to the sociology that lies behind each one.

Chapter Three

THE BIG IDEA TO CHANGE YOUR VIEW OF CHURCH

The Five Contexts of Discipleship

- "Sometimes I find our church services to be deeply frustrating. While there are weeks where I meet with God in worship and find my mind and spirit fed by the sermon, I often have this nagging feeling of, 'Is that it? Is that the best way we can do and be the church?'"

- "I love my small group, but the problem is that people keep bringing new people. I realize that sounds so selfish, but actually I want to stay with a limited number of people, getting to know them deeply over a long period of time. There is this pressure in small group life to invite others in, to help neighbors and friends discover what we have, but by their very joining, what we have is lost, as the group simply becomes too big to properly care for each other."

- "When I read the Bible's descriptions of church life, I have trouble matching that with our pastor's insistence that what we are doing on a Sunday morning is the same thing. For instance, since when was the Lord's Supper meant to be a quick pause for a snack on a nasty cracker and a droplet of grape juice that is being rapidly passed around a big room in virtual silence?"

- "Our church said we had to multiply our home group. It was horrible— all these people I'd grown so close to were now off somewhere else. To me it felt like a divorce, not a celebration."

- "I get annoyed with these people who complain that they don't feel close to everyone in our worship service. What do they expect—we go around the room and ask all 250 people for their prayer requests?"

Whenever people gather, there are so many expectations! Whether it's as a family, with friends, at work, or simply to watch a sports game, multiple agendas are at play.

This range of expectation is taken to a whole new dimension of complexity when the gathering is a church event. While everything in life has a spiritual dimension, when people gather to meet with Jesus, they bring heightened levels of unstated desires, dreams, and needs. In such expectations lie the joys, and frustrations, of church life!

Because the church is in the business of making disciples, all sorts of opportunities are open to us as we encounter these competing demands. If we can help provide contexts where people learn to better listen to Jesus and obey him, their journeys of faith will be deepened and our witness to the world strengthened.

Unfortunately, our preconceived notions of how the church should look when she gathers often inhibit our discipleship. We take our own cultural norms and read them back into the Bible as the only way of doing things, yet it is easy for us to forget that most of what we view as normative came about only through the willingness of previous (and often quite recent) generations of Christians to innovate, whether in their desire to worship Jesus, build community life, or witness to the world.

These tensions are rooted in our humanity. They are not always sinful or wrong, though human sin does affect all of our relationships. Neither do our divergent viewpoints on church life surprise God, since he created us this way. We are dealing with the ways people connect, both with each other and with God, since these are the primary pathways through which disciples are made. It naturally follows that there will be indications across the breadth of human society—his creation—that may point us to some ways forward.

Jesus is Lord of the scientist in the laboratory as much as he is Lord of the pastor in the pulpit.

If we believe that the entire world is God's domain and that Jesus is Lord of the scientist in the laboratory as much as he is Lord of the pastor in the pulpit, then perhaps we can look for clues outside of the traditional literature on church life. This is not to say that we should ditch everything we've known up to now about church; as you will see, we believe that what we are proposing is deeply biblical. At the same time, we believe that we can learn from the insights of the social sciences—as all truth is God's truth!—and even experience some new breakthroughs in our approach to discipleship.

THE SEARCH TO BELONG

When I first read Joseph Myers's book *The Search to Belong*, I knew I'd struck gold! It is one of the most helpful resources on building Christian community—yet it also is deeply indebted to the sociology of how people connect with others in different-sized spaces, or contexts, for gathering.[20]

Published in 2003, Myers's book builds on the work of the pioneering 1960s sociologist Edward T. Hall, who developed a theory based on the relationship between space and culture, calling it Proxemics. Hall suggested that human beings use four different "spaces" to develop communication and connections: public space, social space, personal space, and intimate space. His research focused on the actual physical distance between people in those different environments, and it had obvious implications in areas such as building design and public transportation.[21]

Myers took these innovative ideas and applied them afresh to look at how community is built and how people experience belonging. He explains, "How we occupy physical space—whether through actual real estate (the shopper standing next to my wife and me in the grocery store line) or through more subtle 'spatial language'—tells others whether we want them to belong."[22]

As a Christian, Myers was able to apply some of his learning to church culture, particularly as a tool for assessing why small groups do (and don't) work.

In discussing Myers's work with several friends, what struck me in particular were his insights into how people experience belonging in each of the different spaces he examined. These insights inevitably led us to consider the question: How well is our church using all of these spaces, and in particular the social size (interactions between twenty to seventy individuals)?

Over the past decade, we have played with these ideas in practice,[23] running them through the filter of how and where Jesus disciples us. Bobby and I have made some adaptations as well. We refer to the different gathering sizes as "contexts" rather than "spaces," to provide a more flexible, nonspatial label. We've added an extra context into the mix and have relabeled what Myers calls "intimate space," now calling it the Transparent Context (primarily because in teaching these ideas, several men became distracted by all this talk of intimacy!).

In recent years Joe Myers has become a friend and we have enjoyed some stimulating debate on these matters. He has been a huge help—swapping ideas with us and even teaching with Alex—and we pay tribute to his groundbreaking work that paved the way for this book. If what follows is flawed in any way, we take full responsibility!

THE FIVE CONTEXTS

Let's take a quick look at the Five Contexts, remembering that the following is more descriptive than it is prescriptive:[24]

The Public Context exists where people gather in the hundreds around a shared outside resource. This might be an event (travelers on the same flight), experience (fans at a pop concert), or influence (followers of the same public figure on social media). If the resource is physically present, people will generally be at least 12 feet away from it (think of your distance from the stage if you go to see a play or concert). In this environment the focus is on engaging with the outside resource, rather than building relational depth with others who also happen to be there.

The Social Context is the range between twenty and seventy people, where we share snapshots of who we are and thereby seek to build affinity with others. Myers points out that in this context (think of a backyard grill-out) three things happen: we build neighborly relations (people we can call upon for minor favors), we start to identify those with whom we'd like to become closer friends, and we reveal elements of our identity and our journey. In terms of Proxemics, we will be somewhere between 4 and 12 feet apart. Interestingly, the distance between two people shaking hands is about 4 feet, which in a new relationship is a common preamble to testing the three things Myers lists.[25]

The Personal Context forms in groups of four to twelve, where we feel able to share private information. Think, for instance, of good friends talking over drinks, revealing personal thoughts and feelings about their ongoing lives and relationships. Usually we are 18 inches to 4 feet apart in this context, which is both within comfortable touching distance and close enough to see the other person as they truly are—warts, wrinkles, and all! Such acceptance and physical closeness are representative of the emotional qualities of a relationship in this context, where we experience a genuine depth of friendship.

The Transparent Context is when you are with just one or two others, making a group of two to four people, your closest of relationships. In the Transparent Context, characterized by complete openness and candor, nothing is held back. This echoes the biblical ideal of being "naked and yet unashamed"—an ideal we live out literally in marriage and metaphorically with our best friends. Hall wrote that you are 0 to 18 inches apart in the closest moments of these relationships, noting that at such proximity the other person's flaws seem to fade away (since your eyes can't properly focus on them). This blurring of flaws is a wonderful metaphor for what is going on relationally at these safest depths of human engagement.

The Divine Context represents God's direct interactions with us, his people, at a one-on-one level. Our focus shifts from cultivating relationships with others to being alone with our Creator and Redeemer as he encounters us in our inner world. We delude ourselves if we believe there can be any barriers in this place; indeed, in this context we come face-to-face with our true selves, as reflected in the loving eyes of our heavenly Father. This communion with God in turn equips us to engage more fruitfully in each of the other four contexts.

To summarize, table 1 presents an overview of the various sociological definitions.

Context	Size	Focus	Distance
Public	100s	Engaging with an outside resource	12'+
Social	20–70	Sharing snapshots that build affinity	4'–12'
Personal	4–12	Revealing private information	18"–4'
Transparent	2–4	Living in vulnerability and openness	0"–18"
Divine	Alone with God	Being with your Creator and Redeemer	Inner world

 TABLE 1

Mind the Gap

As you will have noticed, there are some gaps between the different sizes of groups. Certainly these exist in the real world, but they are typically transition phases, when groups are either growing into the next size or subdividing (or shrinking) into smaller contexts.

Whether this change is occurring with intention or haphazardly, these can be painful times, since the previous unifying focus begins to break down. We'll provide some coaching later in the book for navigating through these shifts, but for now recognize that these transition phases do occur. So if you are part of a small group that numbers in the low to mid teens, notice how the Five Contexts will give you a grid to explain why that number feels *less* fruitful now compared to when it was smaller. In a group of this size you are too big to share and recall everyone's prayer requests, but too small to have that sense of an extended community—an environment into which you can easily fold your unchurched friends and neighbors.

You also may have spotted some overlap between the Transparent and Personal Contexts. Sometimes a small group dynamic occurs in a group of as few as four people, though it also can exist in a larger group of very close friends. This is one of those situations where outcomes come into play. You will likely need to talk about what you are trying to achieve as a group, and that will determine what your group will actually "feel" like in practice.

Finally, we want to offer a word of caution. Don't get too hung up on the margins around the edges of the actual numbers. We'll look at this in more detail in the final chapter, but for now just assume that some well-founded sociology backs up the numbers and divisions we are identifying here.

Mental Gymnastics

Throughout life you will encounter situations that seem to blur the boundaries between these different contexts. When you find yourself in such a spot, your mind will "fix" the physical distance to something that feels most comfortable for you. Myers puts it like this: "Our concept of space is largely a matter of perspective; it's in our minds. Humans adjust their definition of space based on surrounding variables."[26]

For instance, when you are sitting on a plane, physically your proximity to the person in the seat beside you will plop you straight into the Transparent Context. Yet you will mentally massage that experience so that you all remain in the Public Context, enabling you to safely ignore the stranger who was randomly assigned to the neighboring seat. In all likelihood you don't share names, you don't talk (other than for courtesy to meet basic needs), and you certainly don't have lingering eye contact at that close range! As Myers notes about these situations, "We may be touching, but we are far from intimate."[27]

Space, meaning the distance between people, operates in two realms simultaneously: the physical and the mental. While the former is fairly obvious, the latter is more hidden and yet, arguably, is more powerful. As Hall recorded, the way we interact in the different contexts is first developed and decided in the head, rather than in the physicality of the context. Thus the consequence is that, as Myers points out, we don't always interact physically the same way—because we determine our approach mentally in advance.

Sometimes, however, these mental gymnastics are unhealthy and can cause the individual to miss the value of that particular context.

For instance, a small church of around forty-five people that gathers on Sundays to worship will almost invariably operate by the rules of the Public Context (which exists for hundreds of people), when actually their reality fits the Social Context (of twenty to seventy people). This "context confusion" may end up inhibiting their ability to grow in size and maturity.

Of course, we also need to account for the fact that different cultures will have variations in how they perceive and express the boundaries between the contexts. Edward Hall was fascinated by these variations as well, and he looked at both Western and non-Western cultures. While he found that the different spaces (to use his label) exist fairly universally, people did perceive the social rules differently. For example, in the Arab world he found that "privacy in a public place is foreign to them. Business transactions in the bazaar, for example, are not just between buyer and seller, but are participated in by everyone. . . . There is no such thing as an intrusion in public. Public means public!"[28]

With this caveat in mind, we still can safely say that the Five Contexts shape every culture to some extent, even if some of the nuances of social norms are expressed differently.

Dysfunction in Each Context

As you learn to recognize the different contexts, you will also be able to spot when people are operating in a dysfunctional manner. The following are just a few examples of this kind of dysfunction in the various contexts:

- *Public.* Sharing private information with the person who has been placed next to you by chance. Simply because they happen to be sitting alongside you does not make them your friend!
- *Social.* Expecting the gathering to be a performance that is consumed, when actually it is built around mutual interaction and shared contribution.
- *Personal.* Revealing to others what was shared in the privacy of the Personal Context.

- *Transparent.* Talking solely about what you do on the outside rather than who you are on the inside. Living this way will torpedo intimacy.
- *Divine.* Thinking that you can engineer or control this context, as if somehow you can hide from Jesus. For instance, when the Holy Spirit prompts you with a question, he is not doing it to gather information!

Another common misconception occurs when you meet someone who is highly competent in the Public Context and you automatically assume that he or she is equally at ease in the Personal or Transparent Contexts. Just because someone comes across as warm and gregarious on a stage in front of hundreds doesn't mean that he or she is good at interacting with individuals in private. If you reflect a little, you will realize that you know many people who are competent in only some of the contexts and not others.

JESUS AND THE CONTEXTS

As you read through this book, you will find plenty of biblical examples illustrating how each of the Five Contexts functions in the journey of discipleship. However, before we go into detail with each context, we want to outline how Jesus used each of the Five Contexts with great wisdom and discernment.

The concentric circles chart (see fig. 6) serves as a summary of how Jesus ministered in the various contexts. Each one is important, but we can see

Jesus used each of the Five Contexts with great wisdom and discernment.

that the smaller the group, the more customized and focused is his discipling of us.

Our introduction of the Divine Context might cause a "pause to ponder" moment for you. After all, we could be implying that Jesus is not really all that present in the other contexts—as if somehow we are taking the omnipresence of God out of all things and creating the very sacred-secular divide that we wrote against a few pages ago!

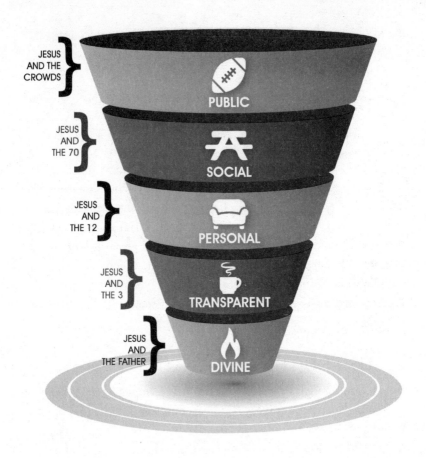

JESUS AND THE CROWDS

JESUS AND THE 70

JESUS AND THE 12

JESUS AND THE 3

JESUS AND THE FATHER

PUBLIC

SOCIAL

PERSONAL

TRANSPARENT

DIVINE

Discipleship•org

>>> FIGURE 6

To clear up any confusion, think of the Divine Context in the following way. There are four contexts in which God disciples us (and invites us to help disciple others) in the everyday reality of simply living life. He is fully present in all of those different situations and relationships. However, we also see an extra context at play, which is somehow different from the other four. It is beyond human interaction, functioning as an overarching environment where we encounter God's presence in such depth that all our human relationships can't help but be impacted. Our level of openness to God when we are alone with him will directly impact

Context	Major Expression	Gospel Passages	What Happened
Public	Jesus and the crowds	Matthew 5:1–2 John 6:1–2 Mark 6:34	Sermon on the Mount Feeding of the 5,000 Compassion for the shepherd-less
Social	Jesus and the 70	Luke 10:1 Matthew 9:9–13 Luke 19	The 70 are sent out Eating with Matthew's tax collector friends Party at the home of Zacchaeus
Personal	Jesus and the 12	John 13 Matthew 8:23–27 Mark 8:27–33	Washing the disciples' feet Calming the storm Confession (and rebuke) of Peter
Transparent	Jesus and the 3	Luke 9:28–36 Mark 10:35–45 Matthew 26:36–38	Transfiguration James and John's request Looking for prayer support at Gethsemane
Divine	Jesus and the Father	Mark 1:35 Luke 6:12 John 5:19	Waking early to pray Before calling the Twelve Jesus does only what he sees the Father doing

 TABLE 2

our fruitfulness in both being discipled and discipling others in the other four contexts.

THE CHURCH AND THE CONTEXTS

Along with these biblical examples from the life and ministry of Jesus, we will examine how discipleship occurs in each context and how it comes to particular expression in church life.

- *Sunday worship services* clearly equate most readily to the Public Context. This is the most common size of church gathering—which leads to the problem of wrongly expecting Sundays to deliver most of our discipling.

- *Missional communities* are the rare, but best, expression of the Social Context in church life. This context is conspicuous by its absence in most churches! Even if you have a group of this number of people, it likely is not bound together by people sharing snapshots of who they are in order to build a common affinity. A missional community is an extended family of relationships, centered around Jesus, that goes and makes disciples among a specific group of people. A lot more detail follows in later chapters!

- *Small groups* are an obvious example of how churches operate in the Personal Context, and clearly these are a widespread expression of Christian life. The pressing issues tend to be that most small groups are allowed to grow too large, thus undermining their original strengths, and if we are honest they usually have little to no real ongoing missional impetus.

- *Deepest friendships, discipleship groups, and marriages* clearly have the ability to reach into the Transparent Context. Most churches do fairly well at encouraging these areas, but they cannot be organized centrally. Your church pastor can't tell you whom your best friend should be or decide whom you should marry (unless they're forming a cult—in which case, run!).

- *Your personal walk* with God is how the Divine Context impacts every one of us. The quality and strength of your relationship with

Jesus will have a direct bearing upon the vitality of the other four contexts. The difficulty, of course, is that it is hard to measure how someone else is truly doing alone with God.

What we want to show, in each of the following pairs of chapters, is that God disciples us in each of the contexts, shaping and molding hearts, minds, and lives—and calling us to imitate his example with those we lead. As we noted at the beginning of this chapter, the key to fruitfulness is to bring the appropriate expectations to each context. Too often people arrive with a tangle of desires and misunderstandings, which short-circuits the blessings and opportunities that the Lord has hardwired into that situation. Over a number of years I have developed three desired outcomes for each of the contexts (which are described in detail in each of the relevant chapters). While the desired outcomes easily could have become a list of ninety-nine things, boiling them down to three core measures of health gives us a powerful evaluative tool.

You will notice immediately that, bar one, these are not lists of actual tasks; they are expressions of measurable values. This is a reflection of the missional nature of your calling: your unique place of mission requires you to express these outcomes in ways that impact the people you are called to disciple. In whatever context you find yourself, you can use the three outcomes to assess and develop that specific situation.

All of the outcomes are summarized in table 3, along with the main points for each of the Five Contexts.

As you look over this list, we want you to see that there are both *stop* and *start* implications that apply personally and to those you lead:

- You must *stop* expecting complete discipling from just one or two contexts.
- You must *start* a sustainable rhythm of church that gives you each of the Five Contexts, thereby enabling you to play your part in discipling others!

How is any of this possible, especially in our crazy-busy lives? That is what we want to show you in this book as we move through each of the contexts in turn, beginning with the Public Context.

Context	Size	Focus	Distance	Learning from Jesus	Church Expression	Outcomes
Public	100s	Engaging with an outside resource	12'	Jesus and the crowds	"Sundays"	Inspiration Movementum Preaching
Social	20–70	Sharing snapshots that build affinity	4'–12'	Jesus and the 70	Missional communities	Community Mission Practice
Personal	4–12	Revealing private information	18"–4'	Jesus and the 12	Small groups	Closeness Support Challenge
Transparent	2–4	Living in vulnerability and openness	0"–18"	Jesus and the 3	Deepest friendships; marriage	Intimacy Openness Impact
Divine	Alone with God	Being with your Creator and Redeemer	Inner world	Jesus and the Father	Personal walk	Identity Destiny Truth

>>> TABLE 3

Chapter Four

THE HOOPLA CAN ACTUALLY WORK

Understanding the Public Context

> **Key Principle:** In the Public Context, over one hundred people are present and discipleship occurs primarily through inspiration, "movementum," and preaching.

PUBLIC

Sam and Jessica were oblivious.

While knots of people busily chatted with friends, and children giggled at the sheer joy of chasing each other over and under the chairs, the young couple could barely talk, let alone move.

Ninety minutes earlier, when they had chosen to sit three-quarters of the way back in the auditorium, neither of them had expected to meet with God quite so profoundly.

For Sam, it had taken place during the worship. At first he had been distracted thinking about the quality of the band, with its enthusiastic if slightly off-tempo drummer. But something had shifted, and God had captured his attention. He had found himself utterly absorbed by an extraordinary awareness of the presence of Jesus. A deep sense of both security and destiny had enveloped him as his vision and perspective of Jesus grew tangibly in what felt like just a few minutes of worship. This was holy ground. Sam knew he would leave the building a different man.

Although she loved to worship, Jessica had been caught unawares by the sermon. The gray-haired preacher had looked so staid and, frankly, dull—until the Bible had been opened in an astonishing manner, with dozens of gems of truth and grace being mined from it. She had been most impacted by the closing challenge: To what are you giving your life? And she knew the Spirit of God had led her through confession into a greater commitment to follow Jesus into the mission field of her workplace, whatever the cost.

Such stories are far from unique. So many of us have been drawn closer to Jesus in the Public Context, where, alongside hundreds or even thousands of other believers, we have encountered the living God.

THE PUBLIC CONTEXT

In the Public Context—groups of over one hundred—we gather around a shared outside resource. It might be an event or an experience, a product or an idea, physical or virtual. The reason we gather is to receive inspiration, an increased movement or momentum (what we term "movementum"), or to be fueled up in some way that is best delivered, or can be best resourced, in a large gathering.

Think back to when you were last at an elementary school concert— that was almost certainly in the Public Context. Whenever you sit at the gate in an airport waiting to board your flight, vote in the candidate selection process of your political party of choice, or contribute to an online forum about your favorite brand of shoe, cell phone, or car, you are operating in this space.

I'm a huge fan of Liverpool Football Club (by the way, that's proper football of the round ball variety!), and so, along with hundreds of thousands of others, I engage with the team in the Public Context. If I meet someone for the first time and they also identify as a Liverpool fan, we have an immediate point of connection and conversation—even though we might never ask each other's name! That is not rudeness if we are operating solely in this space.

While the Public Context is where we are the least self-revealing, that doesn't mean we don't connect with others in meaningful ways. As Joseph Myers has pointed out, we can indeed find a place of belonging in the Public Context, but we first must realize that it will look very different from belonging in the other contexts.[29]

The Public Context arguably has been the central expression of

Christianity in the West during the past seventeen hundred years of Christendom. When most people in Western nations talk about church, they are probably thinking of a Sunday morning service in a large building that anyone can attend. Clearly there are both benefits and drawbacks to this heritage, some of which we will explore, but for now we must make one point clear. Discipleship can indeed happen in the Public Context, as there are certain things it is set up to do exceptionally well.

The key is to help people come with the right expectations for this particular space.

Jesus in the Public Context

Even a quick read through the Gospels reveals that Jesus was a genius at operating in the Public Context. Through signs and wonders, teaching, and the sheer quality of his character, huge crowds were attracted to Jesus during his ministry on earth, and he stewarded those times astutely and wisely.

Jesus' baptism was a fascinating occasion, as he received a profound divine affirmation of his identity and calling, all within a Public Context of huge crowds watching on (Luke 3:21). The Sermon on the Mount commenced when Jesus saw the crowds (Matt. 5:1) and, implicitly, their deep need to understand more about the nature of God's kingdom. And the feeding of the five thousand self-evidently took place in a public space, impacting the crowd's perception of the identity of Jesus (John 6:14). Mark tells us that Jesus was driven by a great compassion for the crowds, "because they were like sheep without a shepherd" (Mark 6:34).

Luke 8:43–48 tells a beautiful story of a woman whom Jesus healed. She had been bleeding for over twelve years, which in Jewish culture would have made her ritually unclean and a social outcast in that town. When she humbly and quietly reached out in faith to touch the edge of Jesus' robe, not wanting to bring attention to herself since she should not have been there, she was indeed healed physically. Yet Jesus wanted to bring holistic healing to her—including her emotions and relationships. Thus we have the gasp-out-loud moment when he calls her out in public and urges her to say both what the problem had been and how she had just been healed. Jesus then affirmed and blessed her, thereby ensuring that the people of the town knew that she was now clean and readmissible into their community life.

At the start of his last few days of ministry before the crucifixion, Jesus entered the temple courts; in front of the crowds and with children racing about all over the place, he drove out the money changers and those who had corrupted the place of worship. He was revealing to all, old and young alike, that the most important thing to our heavenly Father is our open relationship with him, as expressed through the idea of a house of prayer (Matt. 21:12–16).

And in John 7 we see Jesus enter the temple at the height of one of the great festivals and invite the vast crowds to come to him and drink living water. This is a classic example of ministering in the Public Context!

While Jesus regularly and frequently used the Public Context to explain and model discipleship, he was also wise about its limitations. In John 2:23–25 we are told that Jesus would not entrust himself to the crowds because of their sinful nature. While some of that has to do with his messianic identity, more broadly it also reminds us that we should be careful about what we self-reveal publicly.

We should be careful about what we self-reveal publicly.

Public Context ministry is an important part of our receiving, and giving, discipleship. It has a number of amazing strengths, but it carries some potentially huge pitfalls as well.

Public Context Discipleship in the Old Testament

Throughout the Old Testament we witness the ongoing efforts of God to disciple the people of Israel. One of the ways in which this discipleship occurred was through direct interaction with the gathered tribes.

The Ten Commandments (Exodus 20) are a classic example, as God set out some core elements of the call to discipleship. Unfortunately, the response of the nation was to turn them into a list of rules rather than letting them form the basis of a relationship, as they asked Moses to be their go-between with God so that they wouldn't have to hear his voice for themselves (v. 19). They desired precepts over God's presence, and unsurprisingly, within days they had turned from God and built for themselves the golden calf to worship.

Public Context gatherings will quickly take on a religious spirit if they lose sight of the big picture: we gather in order to express and strengthen our personal relationship with God, within the context of the growth of the people of God in number and maturity.

As the people of Israel entered the Promised Land, a number of Public Context times of discipleship took place. The parting of the River Jordan challenged the people to trust God for the miraculous, even when everything around them indicated they would fail. I love the briefing that occurs in Joshua 3:5: "Consecrate yourselves, for tomorrow the LORD will do amazing things among you." He certainly did!

David's defeat of Goliath (1 Samuel 17) reminded the people to trust in God's strength rather than human power, and also laid a foundation for the future kingship of David. In a similar way, Elijah's public humiliation of the prophets of Baal on Mount Carmel (1 Kings 18) called Israel back to faithful worship of the one true God, and at the same time publicly endorsed the ministry of Elijah.

Public worship of God is one of the key themes of the Old Testament, particularly during the reigns of David and Solomon. Both father and son led huge public worship events—when David brought the ark of the covenant into Jerusalem (2 Samuel 6) and later when Solomon led the dedication of the newly completed temple (2 Chronicles 7). Their extravagant, sacrificial exuberance spoke powerfully to the nation about wholehearted devotion to the Lord.

Jumping forward in time, the supernatural appearing of the writing on the wall in King Belshazzar's palace (Daniel 5) showed God's concern to disciple those not currently in his kingdom. The challenge—to demonstrate humility before God, especially regarding the blessings he has bestowed—may have come too late for Belshazzar, but it was part of the foundation for the fruitfulness of Daniel's ministry under subsequent kings.

Public Context Discipleship in the Early Church

You might be surprised to realize that in the book of Acts, the Public Context was not the primary space where God either discipled his people or grew his church. Here is the problem: in contrast to the actual narrative of the New Testament, we have been so conditioned by our culture that we assume the Public Context is self-evidently the primary (even the sole) place for discipleship. As we'll see in later chapters, the Social Context seems to be far more central in the story of the growth of the early church.

Nevertheless, we can still find examples of discipleship taking place in the Public Context. For example, in Acts 2 at the birth of the church, the initial Social Context group rapidly multiplied into a group of three thousand on the day of Pentecost. The text is at pains to show that the church still used homes as the place for building community ("broke bread in their homes," 2:46). However, the church also met in the temple courts for public witness and worship. It is not hard to imagine good news stories from homes and neighborhoods being collected and shared at those larger events, which in turn would give fuel to those street-level communities. Later, after the persecution of the church began, Philip went to previously off-limits towns in Samaria (Acts 8), where large crowds were attracted by the teaching, healings, and deliverance.

As a rapid way to seed a town or region, Public Context gatherings can be highly effective—but we must realize that this is just one part of the journey of discipleship for the individuals in that place.

Paul operated in the Public Context in a number of instances. In the city of Athens he started off by debating daily in the marketplace (Acts 17:17) and eventually received the opportunity to teach at the Areopagus (v. 19), where philosophical and religious ideas were more formally debated. As a trained and gifted orator, Paul utilized those openings to great effect.

A similar pattern emerged in Ephesus, where Paul spent two years debating and discipling in the lecture hall of Tyrannus (Acts 19:9). This work, coupled with some extraordinary miracles—even handkerchiefs and work aprons that Paul had merely touched could heal the sick—sparked a huge change in the spiritual climate of the city, marked by confession of sin and the burning of huge numbers of expensive sorcery scrolls.

These examples all show us that one of the ways God disciples people groups—both those who are committed to him and those who are not currently his followers—is through the Public Context.

And at the End of Time . . .

The book of Revelation gives us some tantalizing glimpses into eternity. We see angels numbering thousands upon thousands encircling the throne of God, declaring the worthiness and honor of Jesus, worship that in turn is echoed by every creature in heaven and on earth (Rev. 5:11–13).

Further on we see "a great multitude that no one could count, from every nation, tribe, people and language, standing before the throne and before the Lamb" (Rev. 7:9). The enormous crowd is engaged in worship of God, a theme that bubbles up throughout the book—see, for example, Revelation 19:1: "After this I heard what sounded like the roar of a great multitude in heaven shouting: 'Hallelujah! Salvation and glory and power belong to our God.'"

We can readily conclude that Public Context worship services, numbering into the millions—maybe billions!—are a part of our heavenly future! What a phenomenal experience that will be!

DISCIPLESHIP IN THE PUBLIC CONTEXT

In the current day, the clearest example of discipleship in the Public Context is the weekly public worship service. Usually held on Sunday morning in a dedicated church building, these gatherings have been a familiar sight in European villages, towns, and cities for many centuries. As settlers from Europe took the gospel to the nations, including the United States, this Sunday-centric model of church life took hold worldwide. Only in countries where Christians experienced ongoing persecution did smaller gathering sizes predominate.

> **Sunday services are not the only way to make disciples in the Public Context.**

As we look back at all that history, we recognize that a lot of great discipleship occurred in those church services. The Bible was taught, God was worshiped, and the bigger picture of the church universal was presented. Lives were changed—and continue to be changed today.

Yet Sunday services are not the only way to make disciples in the Public Context.

A gathering in the hundreds that has Jesus at the center is going to see

Public Context discipleship take place—for instance, an evangelistic rally held in a stadium.

With the advent of our technologically wired society, thousands of people can now connect around a shared resource without physical proximity, and all can experience discipleship. Think about readers of a magazine article, a blog, or even a tweet, or those who are supporters of the same campaigning organization.

Not all of these Public Context discipleship opportunities will be explicitly Christian events. I (Alex) remember being at a U2 concert a few years ago and realizing this truth anew. Tens of thousands of people were in a football stadium for the definitive rock concert—loud, pulsating, and anthemic songs, led by band members who were masters in the art of stagecraft, aided by a thirty-seven-ton claw from which descended a colossal 360-degree video wall. Wow! As fun as that was, two-thirds of the way through we found ourselves in a moment of discipleship, as Bono had us all singing the refrain from "Amazing Grace" before leading into "Where the Streets Have No Name," a song about longing for the fullness of God's kingdom to break out in the world around us today while at the same time hungering for heaven. The audience was being given the opportunity to glimpse the heart of Jesus, and implicitly we were invited to consider our response to Jesus.

So how do we know when authentic discipleship is occurring in the Public Context? The answer is to take a closer look at our expectations and measures of success for this context.

GOALS FOR DISCIPLESHIP IN THE PUBLIC CONTEXT

Public worship services come in a wide variety of styles. Whether our preferred style is highly structured and liturgical, or free-form and relaxed, our assessment about disciple-making effectiveness has to be more biblically grounded than whether we "liked" what went on.

Think of it this way: the value of a newspaper article that points people to Jesus has to be gauged by something more substantial than whether we agree with the political slant of that paper. The same principle can be applied when it comes to social media (more on that later).

At this point I (Alex) have to mention my own experience of watching missional communities grow, multiply several times over, and then desire to reconnect from time to time in a Public Context worship service. These groups naturally want to model a way of "doing worship" that reflects the missional impetus and community life that they've experienced in the Social Context, so the question becomes: What boundaries and what outcomes should we be expecting of those new celebrations?

Often there is a strong temptation to focus on specific activities and tasks and thus create a prescriptive "to do" list. But that is neither a flexible nor a particularly mission-minded model, since it inhibits locally derived, incarnationally driven celebrations of faith. Instead we encourage the focus to shift to outcomes. In Public Context gatherings, what are three core outcomes that will transfer across different cultures and people groups, allowing flexibility in style and taste, yet retaining rigor in values and authenticity to the gospel?

Three words that summarize our expectations or goals for public worship are *inspiration*, *movementum*, and *preaching*.

Goal 1: Inspiration

When we are inspired by Jesus, our gaze is lifted, our hearts are emboldened, our resolve is strengthened, our courage is fueled, our character is purified, and our everyday life is ennobled. There is such tremendous power in inspiration, both to anchor our identity and to call forth our destiny.

In Public Context worship services, we join with hundreds of others in worshiping our crucified and risen Lord Jesus. As all of our voices are raised together in unison, our affections naturally turn toward God as we gaze upon his awesome beauty. Through the energy, enthusiasm, and celebration of the crowd, individuals feel personally drawn close to God during Spirit-filled times of worship.

Or maybe we sit in the stillness of sacred space, aware of the vastness of God—and yet also his closeness. As my gaze is lifted off myself and onto him, I am restored and refreshed in the deepest places. Yet this experience is not mine alone—in the company of others, even though I may never talk with them or know their names, I find a place in the broader people of God.

Our faith in God should be strengthened and renewed during times of public worship. Even if life is tough personally, the worship service is a great place to come meet with God, be filled up with the Holy Spirit, and experience Christ's peace, all alongside fellow travelers on this journey of discipleship.

And while our experience is that the Social Context is most effective at mission, this doesn't mean that mission does not occur in larger worship services. Handled well, the Public Context has the ability to communicate that we are a big family of families and that people can come home and meet with God in this open yet sacred space.

People can come home and meet with God in this open yet sacred space.

Thus we leave more attuned to the presence of God and better able to follow his will as we go about our lives, even in difficult circumstances.

In his classic book *Celebration of Discipline*, Richard Foster writes, "To worship is to experience reality, to touch Life. It is to know, to feel, to experience the resurrected Christ in the midst of the gathered community. It is a breaking into the Shekinah (glory or radiance) of God, or better yet, being invaded by the Shekinah of God."[30]

Another way of thinking about worship in the Public Context is to ask, "Did we leave room for the Holy Spirit?" Whether during the worship songs, the preaching, a story or testimony, or Holy Communion, we must not be afraid to pause and recognize what God is highlighting.

Broader Inspiration

In addition to building the faith of those who come to worship, our Public Context services also serve as a source of inspiration for a broader arena—the watching world.

Many people, for whatever reason, aren't involved in a church but still like the idea that people in their community meet to pray and worship God. They might have all sorts of issues (and flaky theology!) to sort out with God one day, but they also feel that there is an open door for whenever that day comes around.

In the meantime, they might pop in on occasion just to make sure that this is still true. They might be in the crowds at Christmas or Easter, or slip in one day simply to sit in the church sanctuary, or perhaps drop off a donation for a good cause that we publicly support. They have a sense that this is "their" church—which might come as a complete surprise to the regular attenders but is nonetheless true for these individuals. They know that they have, in reserve perhaps, the option of calling upon that church in a time of need. Some of these occasions are obvious—sickness, death, birth, marriage—and then there are those unexpected times of need.

A high school baseball team was preparing—unexpectedly—to go to the state championships. One of the coaches contacted a local church to ask if the pastor would come and pray with the team and share the story of David and Goliath to help prepare the boys for their underdog status!

While the team and coaches numbered in the twenties, this sort of invitation is more of a reflection of a church's Public Context role. This church had built a positive reputation in the community (including serving the high school on many occasions), and so the coach likely didn't view his request as out of the ordinary.

The church pastor was excited that the coach wanted to bring prayer and the sharing of the Bible to the team. And like all good stories, this one had an amazing ending: this local team went on to win the state championships!

The human heart is hardwired to seek profound moments of inspiration that are shared with others. Although our brains are engaged, often these are times where our more creative, intuitive, and artistic sides are being nurtured and discipled. Jesus wants to redeem our whole humanity, and public worship is an important part of this process.

Jesus wants to redeem our whole humanity, and public worship is an important part of this process.

This longing for shared moments of inspiration is part of the attraction of social media: it is played out seemingly in front of the whole world and (when it works well) can be a wonderful experience in which to participate. In a similar way, you know you're in a place of Jesus-centered inspiration when it feels like you're "coming home," when you've entered sacred space and God's presence is there.

Goal 2: Movementum

The kingdom of God is repeatedly pictured in the New Testament as something that undergoes exponential growth and multiplication. The tiniest of seeds becomes the largest of plants, the smallest quantity of yeast works through the whole batch, the five loaves and two fish feed a vast crowd.

Life in the church is meant to have this same sense of rapid change that causes both excitement and godly discomfort! In the Acts of the Apostles, we witness the church regularly taking flying leaps forward, often with the believers being stretched well out of their comfort zone.

It's no coincidence that the stories of the early church were captured and preserved for future generations. Even today, two thousand years later, the long-dead pioneers of the Christian faith speak to us with both encouragement and challenge.

If you are a disciple of Jesus, then you are part of a world-changing movement. Your street, neighborhood, and workplace are at the front lines of all this activity! Yet you may be prone to forget this truth and to feel that your situation is either neglected by God or uniquely prioritized by him.

When we gather in public worship services, one of our goals should be the building of "movementum." This made-up word combines the sense of both movement and momentum to describe an organic, rapidly repro-ducing expression of God's kingdom.[31] That might sound like something very distant from your own experience, but part of the value of the Public Context is that we gain a glimpse of how our little local efforts are playing a part in this wider movementum.

Thus our public worship services should be full of stories of what God is up to in the different lives and missional communities that are repre-sented there. As we listen to these accounts, we gain a wider and deeper perspective. We perceive how our personal story fits into the bigger story of what God is doing in our area, which in turn fits into the big story of how the kingdom is advancing across the world today, and ultimately all these stories are gathered up within the overarching Story of God across time and space. We gain perspective on the far-reaching movement of

God, which gives fresh impetus and momentum to our own local efforts, and thus movementum is produced.

Through the telling of people's stories and the celebration of our community heroes (for every organization has its own hero system of people who are held up as examples of how we should live in accord with our shared values), we can build a dynamic movement.

More broadly, we should be asking ourselves whether what we do in our public gatherings is fueling our larger mission of discipleship. The stories and videos we share, the events we promote, the leaders we commission, the occasions we celebrate, the specific challenges we issue, the clear steps we invite people to take—all should serve our broader disciple-making strategy that takes place throughout the week.

All healthy, Jesus-centered Public Context gatherings will feature the telling of stories that increase movementum. And while stories are a key expression of movementum, the real win is that people leave both encouraged and equipped to move forward with greater energy, boldness, and focus.

Goal 3: Preaching

Biblical preaching is hugely important in the diet of a disciple. We need a place where gifted men and women can open up the Bible, bringing to the gathered crowd a "now" word of God that is firmly rooted in Scripture. To make this happen, we need to identify those who have the character, competency, and calling to perform this task, so that we can enable them to set aside the time to prepare sermons for public worship services.

Clearly there will be a vast range of styles and preferences in the way sermons are delivered and responded to, but certain core characteristics will resonate across the spectrum. Many books have been written on this topic, and some common themes emerge. We will need to engage properly with the biblical text, lift Jesus high in the message, share the gospel, and seek a clear response from those listening. We'll also need to think about our listeners' hearts, making sure their minds and lifestyles are being both encouraged and challenged, and seeking, as the preacher, to have a winsome and engaging manner that is clearly Spirit led.

Let's think for a moment about *why* preaching works best in the Public Context.

For starters, it's not personal! When speaking to a crowd in the hundreds, the preacher is bound to say things that resonate deeply at a personal level. Yet the very fact that such a large group is listening means that these are not personally aimed comments, and so the hearer is better able to acknowledge God speaking to their own situation. By *not* being personalized, preaching can be highly personal!

In addition, difficult topics and taboos can be tackled. Enough people are in the Public Context that hot-button issues can be taught with a level of explicitness that would be awkward to sit through in a smaller group size. Remember, in the Public Context people gather primarily for the shared outside resource rather than for the social interaction. Thus, for example, a candid talk on sexuality will be more easily heard in the Public Context.

Core content (or vision) can be shared with a large number of people in the Public Context. This central teaching can then be more specifically applied and lived out in the other contexts, creating an efficient framework for building unity in our diversity.

Another advantage of preaching in the Public Context is that people are not forced into a response. While the preacher should seek a response from listeners, in a group of hundreds of people there is never one sole anticipated outcome. A variety of responses (both positive and negative) can be expected in this size of gathering; by contrast, the smaller the context, the greater the social pressure for a fairly overt and uniform response.

Finally, at this scale anonymity is assured. As long as the leaders of the worship service are honoring the rules of the Public Context, it is perfectly fine to remain anonymous in this size of gathering. This means, for instance, that those with doubts can just listen in and process what they hear at their own pace. In the Public Context, no one really notices if someone is not paying attention. Before you raise your voice in horror, be honest—there are plenty of times when you have tuned out some (or all) of a sermon! In the Public Context such tuning out can take place without causing social awkwardness (well, until the person on the front row starts snoring loudly, as happened to me in the first church I served!). While

I'm not encouraging idle daydreaming during the preaching, sometimes it may be that the Lord is speaking to a person uniquely as they sit in his presence with a Bible open in front of them. Other times it may just be a case of allowing people to be people and not expecting them to be perfect all the time.

Preaching in the Public Context is an important part of our growth as disciples of Jesus. Through these times we receive teaching that will fuel our discipleship journey as we go back out to our places of mission.

Now that our core outcomes have been established—inspiration, movementum, and preaching—we can dig deeper into the ways discipleship can be developed in the Public Context.

Chapter Five

WHAT THE BIG DOES WELL

Discipleship in the Public Context

Key Application: Shape your big gatherings so that people leave encouraged and equipped to better represent Jesus in their everyday lives.

A member of the welcome team at our church sent me (Alex) the following story recently:

On a recent Sunday, a teacher at an inner-city school approached me at the Welcome Center. She asked if we had any Bibles to give away and proceeded to tell me about how she weaves her faith into the classroom.

Recently she had a couple of students notice her Bible on the desk. As she talked with the students, she recognized that they were open to hearing about Jesus and she wanted to have some Bibles available to give away.

That day I gave her a half dozen Bibles. She understood the need to be careful not to abuse her position of authority, but also realized that if students asked about Jesus then she wanted to be able to respond properly.

Her inspiration for taking this step had come directly out of the preaching that morning, which was about being willing to be a representative of Jesus wherever we go, including our places of work.

In a Public Context gathering, this teacher was impacted by the sermon and prompted to take an immediate next step. The size of the public worship service enables us to reach a large number of people with a clear challenge and invitation. And to follow up on people's responses to these calls to action, the public gathering operates at a scale whereby it makes good stewardship sense to keep resources on hand (such as a stock of Bibles to give away).

DON'T VIOLATE THE RULES OF THE PUBLIC CONTEXT

The outcomes we looked at in the previous chapter—inspiration, movementum, and preaching—summarize what a Public Context gathering will do well. In other areas, however, it won't perform as strongly.

To help you think this through, here's a real-life example. See if you can spot why this suggestion won't work. It's from a blog post that listed ideas for how to increase hospitality in the church.

> *10. Encourage members to greet new people.*
>
> If you attend a large church it is hard to know everyone. But regardless of the church size try encouraging those who have attended for a while to introduce themselves to someone they don't know.
>
> If you want to take a risk here, rather than have a 10-second handshake time try allowing 2–5 minutes for people to introduce themselves and find a way they can pray for someone sitting near them.

The author invites us to take a risk here—and it really is just that! Why is this well-intended suggestion such a bad idea? The issue is that all this handshaking, talking, and praying completely violates the rules of the Public Context. People are not just being asked but arevirtually compelled to share private information with people they don't know. For introverts this is pretty close to the perfect definition of a waking nightmare! And to be honest, most extroverts would be highly uncomfortable with this exercise as well.

One of the keys to discerning what works best in public worship services is to reflect on the descriptions of the different contexts. In the Public Context we gather around shared resources, whereas the Personal Context is where we share private information. Taking time to find a way to pray for someone is excellent—when done in the right context. In this case, it should take place in a group of four to twelve, where everyone has made the conscious decision to enter into the social contract of a group of that size. When someone comes to a public worship service, they expect it to be governed by the rules of that context. To ignore those rules will massively undermine your integrity and make the church feel like an unsafe environment.

(Yes, I realize that there are exceptions to any rule, but extreme circumstances are just that—extreme and unusual. The suggestion cited earlier is clearly geared toward a regular worship service.)

When someone comes to a public worship service, they expect it to be governed by the rules of that context.

I recall being a student and visiting a friend's church. After the opening time of worship, the pastor stood up and rather bossily instructed all of the new people to raise their hands. That was pretty awkward, although it was a relief to see there were a few of us naïve lambs scattered around the room.

There followed a long pause, and then at some mystical unannounced command, the regulars stood as one, turned to face the nearest new person, and, with a helpful pitching note from the piano, began to sing a song of welcome to us.

Individually.

In the name of Jesus.

It was as if a weird and creepy horror movie had been created by the makers of *VeggieTales*—a jolly tune and some sweet smiles, which masked a seriously bizarre community.

After what seemed like twenty minutes, the song ended and the congregation sat down, most of them looking about as relieved as I felt. We newbies glanced anxiously across the room at one another, with a shared expression of horror in our eyes. "What on earth just happened here?" went the unsaid question.

The people were friendly and well-meaning, but what was so wrong about that experience?

Well, now you can offer an answer: it was a colossal violation of the rules of the Public Context!

THE CENTER SERVES THE EDGE

As you seek to use the Public Context as a place of discipleship, you will need to make several shifts in the way you prioritize public worship services.

The first issue to tackle is that in many traditional churches the pivotal event of the Christian week is the Sunday service, with the mountaintop being reached as the pastor steps into the pulpit. Please don't misunderstand: as we've already shown, Bobby and I love and greatly value biblical preaching. However, the church's health should not be measured primarily by how many people we can persuade to come in and hear the sermon. Too many churches set themselves up so that the people and ministries are there to serve the vision and ministry of the senior pastor. In other words, the edge serves the center.

By contrast, a church that is focused on making disciples who in turn make disciples will evaluate the church's health differently. For this kind of church, the gifts and ministry of the senior pastor and the staff team are there to resource and equip the wider church body. Instead of the discipling impetus resting with just a few people at the center, it is released to many people on the missional edge of the church, where they intersect with the unchurched in their neighborhoods and networks of relationships. The central resources of the church—staff, finances, ministries, public worship services—are focused on glorifying Jesus by continually fueling and equipping people to go and make disciples wherever God has placed them. In this environment, the center serves the edge.

For the weekend public services, this means that the stories we tell, the illustrations we share, and the sermon applications we make are heavily geared toward encouraging and equipping the hearers to better make disciples throughout the rest of the week.

The Public Context becomes a place where people experience inspiration to keep serving Jesus, a sense of movementum as they see how their local stories fit into a bigger story, and a scriptural refueling that shows how all these stories are wrapped up into the grand Story of God.

THE IDOL OF PERFECTIONISM

The second issue to address in discipleship-focused public worship services is the idol of excessive excellence, or perfectionism.

We no longer live in a churched culture, so we need to start thinking like missionaries who are sent out into the world to bring the kingdom of God wherever we encounter those hungry for the presence of God. Yes, we will still gather back together to worship our risen Savior and Lord, to share stories from the mission frontier, and to be equipped to go back out in his name. But we will do so in a more organic way so that we can maximize the resources we are pouring into mission.

Too many churches dump way too high a percentage of their resources into the Public Context gatherings. I've talked with senior pastors who have been shocked to realize more than 75 percent of their church's resources went toward making the weekend services ever more excellent. While an emphasis on first-rate planning and programming can create some fun events, it makes the church lopsided. If all five of the contexts of discipleship are to be developed properly, we have to move away from this type of perfectionism.

Just to be clear, focusing on making disciples 24-7 is not an excuse to give God sloppy, shoddy, second-rate offerings. At the same time, giving him a precious offering of worship doesn't mean everything has to be perfect. To help you hit the middle ground—great public worship services that don't digress into the perfectionism that reduces the resources (time, energy, focus, prayer, money, staff) available to mission—you need a shorthand evaluative phrase. So instead of "Is this excellent?" how about, "Is this good enough?"

> Being good enough is neither the unbridled pursuit of excellence that leads to perfectionism, nor the lazy apathy that leads to an unacceptable offering.

Being good enough is neither the unbridled pursuit of excellence that leads to perfectionism, nor the lazy apathy that leads to an unacceptable offering. Exactly where this marker of "good enough" falls will depend on your place of mission. In the scope of your ministry, is this good enough in the cultural context of the people you are trying to disciple? Don't forget: good enough in suburban Ohio will look different from good enough in downtown Las Vegas, which in turn will be different from good enough in urban Mumbai or in the Amazon jungles of Peru.

One indicator of having understood good enough is whether what your church does is reproducible by others. If your template can be copied only by rock stars with a pantechnicon full of physical resources, then you are in trouble! An overemphasis on superior technology or showy stage-craft will inhibit you from building a movement that can be multiplied into a variety of contexts. However, aiming for good enough—neither perfectionism nor laziness—creates a model that can be taken and applied wherever the Lord gives you growth.

SOCIAL MEDIA AND THE PUBLIC CONTEXT

I (Alex) love social media! I was an early adopter of Facebook, use Twitter often, and have a presence on many of the other platforms. But social media is still a new world that creates some very particular rules for surviving and thriving within it. The sociology behind the Five Contexts provides a game-changing perspective for all social media users.

I want to suggest that most of our social media interactions fit within the Public Context. You may be surprised to hear that, but stop and consider for a moment.

When you use social media, you may *feel* like you are interacting at an individual level, hearing what someone is doing in their personal life. "Surely that must be the Personal or even Transparent Context?" To which the answer is an emphatic "No!" Everything on social media takes place in front of a large audience. You may be sharing personal snapshots of your life, but unless you are very silly, you do so with the full awareness that hundreds of others are looking on. This is not a Social Context gathering; it is a much larger space where you have very little control over who is listening in (or who will reshare what you have just posted).

Most of our social media interactions fit within the Public Context.

Even if you don't have many "friends," most of what you post on social media is readily searchable and discoverable by others. Like a church of thirty people that holds a public worship service, everyone there is operating by the rules of the Public Context. What you have gathered around is an outside resource—in this case a web-based tool for sharing photos, gossip, news, and interesting ideas.

Consequently, you need to understand the boundaries of appropriate usage of social media. Since it operates within the Public Context, you should be authentic while being fully aware that *this is not the place for genuinely private thoughts and feelings.* Social media is the town square, not your bedroom. As a friend recently commented, "My pillow talk is now available to the world. And I invite the world to my pillow talk."

Not a good idea at all.

Moreover, because of its public nature, social media is not the place for debating strongly held but controversial political or religious beliefs. You are not engaging with individuals in the Personal Context, where it is appropriate to reveal private thoughts and feelings. Rather, you are in the Public Context, where belligerent sharing of beliefs simply serves to annoy or alienate others and makes you look narrow-minded and rude.

As a parent of any teenager today will tell you, there is an art to learning how to interact in a godly manner on social media. The Five Contexts help us understand *why* this is the case.

Of course, this doesn't mean we can't share our faith online. (I do daily.) However, we need to do so in the spirit of Public Context preaching (see above) rather than with the view that we are engaging in a private conversation in which we are relationally looking someone in the eye and having healthy dialogue.

POLITICS, POWER, AND THE PUBLIC CONTEXT

In *Launching Missional Communities*, I wrote about how the church often misunderstands how to engage in debate in the Public Context (or, as I termed it then, public space):

> In public space, we see an open encounter between two kingdoms. Often, though, the church in America either has abandoned this territory or misunderstood what this means in practice. The

journey of modernity into post-modernity has squeezed faith in Christ out of the public space, or discourse, assigning faith to smaller spaces (ideally, faith remains just a "personal and private" thing).

In response to this, many Christians assert that the Gospel is a public message, but wrongly assume that this means that the church should run the government and direct all public policy.

We would do well to learn from the early Christians (and the parallel journey of the modern-day Chinese church), who responded to the Roman state's idolatrous declaration of Caesar as lord by declaring that "Jesus is Lord." Yet they did so from the margins of society, operating as yeast, infiltrating every aspect of the culture without resorting to the tools of the system (high control of society and being the dominant voice in the land). The 1,700-year experience of much of Christianity since becoming legal in the Roman Empire—where the church gradually became synonymous with the state and owned the tallest and best buildings in town to prove its status—is a salutary lesson in correctly aligning our interaction with public space.[32]

The Public Context is a place where we need to learn to operate as Christians, but we must do so wisely, understanding the limits that constrain how we communicate there. I love politics and the political process, and I believe it is vital to have Christians serving at all levels of the political realm. However, we need to engage certain discussions with wisdom and ensure that we are genuinely making disciples of Jesus rather than disciples of worldly power.

HOW DOES ACCOUNTABILITY WORK IN PUBLIC CONTEXT GATHERINGS?

By its very nature, accountability is something that works best in the smaller contexts. The Bible tells us to confess our sins to one another—but this injunction is far more easily, and appropriately, lived out with just one or two others. Can you imagine doing this in a public worship service every Sunday morning?! As noted, such a practice would be a complete violation of the rules of the Public Context.

Yet accountability can operate within the Public Context—it just needs to be set up in a way that works in that type of gathering.

The anonymity of being part of a group of hundreds of people means that individuals can make personal responses to Christ without feeling that they are being personally identified. For instance, some form of altar call—whether it involves standing by your seat, kneeling at the communion rail, or walking to a specified point in the building—allows these personal responses to occur, as long as private information is not shared publicly and a number of other people are able to choose to follow the same path. The very fact that people have gathered around a shared outside resource (in this case, the worship service) means that individuals will sense the cloak of relative anonymity and thus respond to a call to which they would not respond in a Social Context gathering.

If you are organizing Public Context gatherings, you are wise to recognize what this environment does well. People will respond as part of a crowd because, ideally, you have mined a space for them to meet privately with Jesus in the midst of the crowd. For many, it will be a hugely significant experience, one they wouldn't have the spiritual maturity to pursue under their own steam.

Nevertheless, remain aware of the "rules" of the Public Context. For instance, never press people to reveal private information in this environment, unless they can genuinely choose to do so without feeling pressured. And when someone decides to share a story during a service, they should do so with a keen awareness of the environment and what is, and isn't, appropriate for the situation.

CYNICISM AS A BLOCK TO PUBLIC CONTEXT DISCIPLESHIP

Sadly, many people have had bad experiences of church life, especially in the Public Context. Promises were offered that were not kept, demands were made that seemed unreasonable, priorities were set that felt ungodly.

Others have equally jaundiced views of big church gatherings, but which were caused by the church behaving entirely appropriately. Sinful behavior in their life was challenged, the all-or-nothing call of the gospel was too clearly presented, the need to submit our finances to Christ was taught.

Whatever the reason, warranted or not, a number of your friends and neighbors will feel burnt by public worship services. As these friends start to reconnect with the church through missional communities or your personal witness, this cynicism will start to manifest itself afresh.

> **A number of your friends and neighbors will feel burnt by public worship services.**

While part of your task is to listen and help them process their experiences, ultimately this mindset does need to be challenged. Whether through story, teaching, or simply the sharing of your own journey, you can help them understand that resentment and cynicism are not appropriate responses to hold on to. Part of the way you can do this is by talking positively about the strengths of the Public Context. In other words, tie expectations to appropriate outcomes. For instance, you can speak of the power of worshiping Jesus with many others, but don't start promising how close they are going to feel to everyone there, because that outcome simply isn't deliverable.

HOW TO MAXIMIZE THE PUBLIC CONTEXT AS A PLACE OF DISCIPLESHIP

Stop and reflect for a moment. How do you tend to evaluate the success of a public worship service? Is your filter primarily summarized by the question, "What am I getting out of this?"

If that is your approach, you will need to recalibrate your perspective so that you begin to see the public worship service as a place of discipleship. Jesus *can* meet with you powerfully in this context, and you *should* expect to hear what he's saying to you and determine what you are going to do in response. To help you down this pathway, here are a few practical tips:

- Choose to throw yourself into corporate worship. Stop worrying about what everyone around you is thinking about your singing voice (they're actually worrying about how they sound to you!) and focus on honoring and adoring the Lord Jesus.

- Come ready to hear (and share) stories from your church family. Allow them to encourage you where you are healthy and also to stir up a godly thirst for things you aren't yet experiencing.

- Be hungry to grow closer to Jesus through the preaching. This hunger is a choice! Pray for the person who will be speaking. Ask God to speak through them to the church corporately, to your family, to specific friends, and to you personally. If you find your mind wandering during the sermon, ask the Holy Spirit to help keep you focused. Come prepared—bring a Bible (digital or hard copy) and a pen and pad for taking notes. While the worship space is not a classroom, writing down key points does help you engage and absorb a greater quantity of what you are hearing. Also you can record specific applications or nudges the Holy Spirit is making to you directly.

- Expect to respond to what God is doing that day—both during the service and later as you take what you have learned and experienced back out into your everyday life.

- Don't expect the public worship service to be a gathering where you feel a strong sense of community and closeness. No, we won't sing "Happy Birthday" to your friend, even if they are turning twenty-one, forty, fifty, or whatever! (My only exception to this rule is if someone is turning one hundred—there you go, that's something to aim for!) That type of closeness is lived out in the Social Context—more on that in the next chapter.

Don't expect the public worship service to be a gathering where you feel a strong sense of community and closeness.

- The public worship service is not your spiritual pinnacle of the week! It is an important part of your spiritual walk, but discipleship occurs throughout your life, day by day, hour by hour, in all five of the contexts of discipleship.

HOW TO DISCIPLE OTHERS IN THE PUBLIC CONTEXT

Of course, we also need to adjust our self-focused expectations and understand that discipleship is not just about how you or I can grow. As members of the body of Christ, we all have a responsibility to help others grow as disciples of Jesus. This responsibility starts with recognizing that you have opportunities to disciple others in and around public worship gatherings.

First, know that your attitude is infectious. If you come grumpy, grudgingly, and with little expectation of meeting Jesus, that outlook will spread to those around you. So choose your attitudes wisely—they have far greater impact than you realize.

Remember that what you model to those around you, especially to those younger in years or in faith, will be noticed and copied. For example, how do you engage in worship? Hands in pockets, looking bored and not singing, or hands raised, focusing on Jesus and contributing fully to the gathering's worship?

While the Public Context is not characterized by a sense of closeness, that doesn't mean you should be rude and ignore people! The exact opposite is true. Who can you welcome or point in the right direction or serve in a simple way? Will you scoot up your row of seats to allow some latecomers to sit on the end? (That's a crazy-big ask!) People still need to feel like they belong in the Public Context, and you can go a long way toward making that happen.

Finally, be looking out for those you do know. Be ready with an encouraging word, an arm around a shoulder, or simply a high five to celebrate something that's going well. Being part of a huge group worshiping Jesus, growing in excitement as you hear what God is doing in the bigger picture, digesting anointed biblical preaching—all these things will feed your ability to hear what Jesus is saying and to respond as a faithful child of God.

GETTING STARTED

1. (For church leaders:) Gather your key leaders and determine the three core outcomes that are best accomplished in the weekend gatherings at your church. How will you know when you are doing these things well, yet without slipping into perfectionism?

2. In your context, how do people demonstrate that they are being inspired by God? How do they respond to that inspiration? Whether or not you are a church leader, how can you play your part in building a culture that expects the inspiration of meeting with Jesus?

3. What can you do specifically to build the sense of movementum at your public worship services? What can you do similarly through social media?

4. Does anything need to change in the way your community handles preaching, particularly if it is one of the key outcomes of your public worship? Think about not just the content but also the practicalities, mechanics, evaluation, and ways people are called to respond.

ADDITIONAL RESOURCES FOR THE PUBLIC CONTEXT

Ferguson, Dave. *The Big Idea: Focus the Message, Multiply the Impact.* Grand Rapids: Zondervan, 2007.

Kauflin, Bob. *Worship Matters: Leading Others to Encounter the Greatness of God.* Wheaton, IL: Crossway Books, 2008.

Kirkpatrick, Rich. *The Six Hats of the Worship Leader.* CreateSpace Independent Publishing Platform, 2014.

Malm, Jonathan. *Unwelcome: 50 Ways Churches Drive Away First-Time Visitors.* Los Angeles: Center for Church Communication, 2014.

Stanley, Andy. *Communicating for a Change.* Sisters, OR: Multnomah, 2006.

Chapter Six

THE MISSING LINK

Understanding the Social Context

> **Key Principle:** In the Social Context, twenty to seventy people relate and connect, and discipleship occurs through community, mission, and practice.

SOCIAL

Al, Chris, and their young children lived in a town six or seven miles from their church's main building. For a long time they had felt a call, both persistent and consistent, to reach the people of Canal Fulton—friends, neighbors and families, teachers from the schools, servers in the restaurants, leaders of the community, walkers on the towpath, retirees and their grandchildren. The call was to make disciples of anyone and everyone who called that place home.

Al and Chris had discovered that for every person from the town who would accept an invitation to join them in their commute to the church's weekend services, there were many more for whom either the distance or the big service was none too appealing. Increasingly they knew that they needed a different sort of missional strategy if they were going to reach their place of calling.

One Sunday afternoon a few similarly minded families from the church found themselves gathering at Al and Chris's home. As they shared food, conversation, and prayer, they committed to planting a new missional community in their town. Very quickly invitations started to go out to unchurched friends and family in Canal Fulton, and people began turning up on Sunday afternoons at this organic, relational, local expression of church. The group grew—a dozen became twenty-five, which grew to forty, then sixty, then over seventy adults and children were cramming into their small home.

The missional community rapidly multiplied into three groups, and within eighteen months of first starting there were six fully functioning missional communities within Canal Fulton. Along the way, Al and Chris realized that the groups would benefit from regularly gathering together in a Public Context expression of church life, and so a Sunday celebration service began in a local school. The focus of this larger gathering was clear: it existed to fuel, resource, and give thanks for what God was doing through the various missional communities in their town.

Not wanting to settle there, the team around Al and Chris had noticed that a number of those joining the missional communities had experience working in coffee shops, including a former regional manager for Starbucks. Their attention was drawn to this curious fact in a deeper way after they carried out an extensive survey of Canal Fulton asking what would most improve the town. One unexpected response stood out head and shoulders above any other option: the residents of Canal Fulton wanted a decent coffee shop where people could gather and meet. This young team came up with a business plan to open a coffee shop, and they found the perfect downtown location—a 120-year-old building that during Prohibition had been the town brothel and an illegal drinking den! Naturally enough, the name of this new coffee shop was The Speakeasy.

The layout of The Speakeasy was designed using the insights of the Five Contexts. A coffee shop is a perfect example of a Social Context space, which naturally breaks down into the Personal Context at each table. While the coffee shop is not explicitly run as a Christian enterprise to keep it safe and open for the entire town, neither is the church hidden away. After hours, The Speakeasy is the perfect space to host missional community gatherings, and when it is open it is ideal for hosting events that townspeople can simply drop by and enjoy.

While not all missional communities will see such rapid growth or multiplication, this example illustrates the power of a community on a common mission together. As an "extended household" of faith, looking outward to the surrounding town or region is a simple, biblical, and effective way of making disciples from the unchurched community around them—and it can lead to some amazing and unexpected opportunities. Our experience is that the Social Context provides a natural place for people to experience authentic community, join in a common mission, and share their gifts as everyone contributes and lives out their faith.

THE SOCIAL CONTEXT

In the Social Context—a group size of twenty to seventy people—we connect with others by sharing snapshots of what it would be like to be close friends. Through small talk, socializing, and neighborly relations, we reveal enough about ourselves to build authentic community. Many have noticed that the Social Context is typically the place where individuals feel the greatest sense of affinity for one another. It is here that we self-identify as being part of a larger group.

This is our extended family, our network of friends, those from whom we gain a sense of shared identity.

> **The Social Context is typically the place where individuals feel the greatest sense of affinity for one another.**

One of the reasons for this congeniality has to do with the dynamics of group size. There is something significant about this twenty- to seventy-person size range. A group this size is small enough that we can reasonably expect to know each person—their name, temperament, obvious strengths and weaknesses, and role in the community. These specifics form the basis for our mutual support, interactions, and life together.

At the same time, the Social Context is large enough that we can find diversity, common interests, and a shared mission, all of which pave the way for our engagement with the wider world as we acknowledge that the whole (of the group) is greater than the sum of its parts.

As we mentioned earlier, we believe that the Social Context, as an aspect of church life, is best expressed through the planting, development, and multiplication of missional communities.

Jesus in the Social Context

At first, you might wonder how Jesus utilized the Social Context. After all, a great deal of Bible study has focused on Jesus' interactions with either the Twelve (or the three) or the crowds. Yet if we scratch just beneath the surface of the Gospels, we soon discover that he had a high level of competency in Social Context gatherings.

Jesus had a wider band of up to seventy-two followers who were with him enough that he felt comfortable commissioning them to go out and represent him. Luke 10 records Jesus' mandate to the group and their subsequent return with stories of God's power working through them. Jesus' response is interesting: Luke 10:18 records him joyously explaining the spiritual breakthrough that was won by the group of this size being faithful on mission. The Bible indicates that he primarily viewed them not as working in pairs but rather as a group of seventy-two. One take-away is clear: there is tremendous spiritual potency in releasing gangs of missionaries on this scale.

We know that alongside the twelve named male disciples was a larger support network of disciples. Many of these were women, some of them wealthy enough to provide generously for Jesus' Social Context community. Luke 8:1–3 names some of these significant figures who clearly played a vital role in the mission. Many of the passages that we read as referring to the Twelve actually refer to this wider circle of friends and disciples. For instance, Mark 2 explains how a Sabbath walk through the fields drew the ire of the Pharisees, as some of Jesus' disciples were caught plucking heads of grain. This account comes *before* the calling of the Twelve, and the strong implication is that the Pharisees are accompanying Jesus and his gang. (Otherwise they wouldn't have spotted the disciples way out in a field selecting their snacks!)

The Bible portrays Jesus hanging out with a Social Context–sized group, modeling what it means to be a child of the Father. He was (and is!) more than comfortable with people lingering on the edge and patiently allowed them to watch and decide whether they wished to move in closer toward the center.

Even when Jesus named the core twelve disciples, Luke highlights that they came from a wider group: "One of those days Jesus went out to a mountainside to pray, and spent the night praying to God. When morning came, he called his disciples to him and chose twelve of them, whom he also designated apostles" (Luke 6:12–13). Notice this passage tells us he "called his disciples to him" and out of this existing group of disciples (the Social Context) he called the Twelve.

Jesus loved to eat with the spiritually hungry, whatever their history or background. Mark 2:15 tells us, "While Jesus was having dinner at Levi's house, many tax collectors and sinners were eating with him and his disciples, for there were many who followed him." These "sinners and tax collectors" were part of his Social Context, along with the "many" who followed him.

> **Jesus loved to eat with the spiritually hungry, whatever their history or background.**

Don't you love this about Jesus? He is accepting and welcoming of anyone who is interested in finding out more about him. The Social Context was perfect for this kind of interaction—whether on a walk or over a meal. We'll look more at the advantages of the Social Context later, but first notice how often eating a meal is tied to this space where groups of twenty to seventy connect.

Jesus' openness and inclusion had the added benefit of enabling him to disciple the religious types as they reacted in shock to seeing the spiritually outcast being welcomed in. Luke 19 records Jesus' transformational impact on Zacchaeus. Initially Jesus encounters him in the Public Context, then continues to disciple him in the Social Context over dinner with his household (or *oikos*—see below for explanation of this Greek term), no doubt with all his crooked cronies in attendance. Check out the hilarious comment in verse 7: "All the people saw this and began to mutter, 'He has gone to be the guest of a sinner.'" But what did they expect the friends of Zacchaeus to be like? Christ, of course, didn't care—and Jesus models for everyone the power of eating and socializing in the journey of discipleship.

Another beautiful illustration of this principle occurs in Luke 7:36–50, when Jesus, invited to eat at the home of Simon the Pharisee, is followed into the room by a woman who was a renowned sinner. She proceeds to weep all over Jesus and wash his feet with her hair—a scandalous outrage in that culture. Yet around that meal table Jesus was able to disciple the woman into the truth that would set her free, and to disciple Simon and his friends toward the true nature of grace.

Another remarkable Social Context story is when the children are brought to Jesus for his blessing. The twelve disciples try to turn them away—but Jesus, famously, has a different perspective on the value of the next generation. While the text doesn't say exactly how many were there, I picture this scene with several dozen kids swarming around, being corralled closer to Jesus by parents hungry for God's blessing upon their children. Maybe you see it differently, but certainly the Social Context is an excellent-sized gathering for discipling children and teens.

Finally, Jesus also experiences the pain of rejection in the Social Context. Matthew 13 ends with Jesus teaching in the synagogue at his hometown of Nazareth—a group of twenty to seventy people. While there, his former neighbors and friends work themselves up into a lather of righteous indignation at the spiritual authority Jesus is exercising, returning to their favored narrative of his scandalous conception and birth. The people's stinging rejection had all the more bite because it happened in this smaller-sized gathering. When you are rejected for your commitment to Christ, know that Jesus truly understands what you are going through.

Other Biblical Examples

The story of Moses gives us a range of examples of discipleship in each of the Five Contexts. The Social Context is less obvious, but it is still present in his life. We see it highlighted as Moses wrestles through the burden of leading such a large and difficult group of people. Numbers 11 tells us about the seventy elders of Israel who were called by God to come alongside Moses as a leadership community. As Moses discipled them, they in turn were equipped to go and lead a wider circle of leaders.

As they gathered around a meal, God discipled the leaders of the community.

Exodus 24:9–11 provides a delightful picture of God revealing himself to all seventy of the elders along with Moses and Aaron. They saw God face-to-face, yet "God did not raise his hand against these leaders of the Israelites; they saw God, and they ate and drank" (v. 11). As they gathered around a meal, God discipled the leaders of the community.

Many other examples from the Old Testament show how discipleship happened in the Social Context. For instance, we can see:

- The influence of Daniel among the wise men and magicians of Babylon.
- The comfort and solidarity brought to David by his band of mighty men. This is a great example of a Social Context group, bound together in community with a common mission and the space for everyone to play their part, enabling new leaders to emerge.
- The strength given to Jacob by his family accompanying him on the move to Egypt.

While the Bible includes many such examples and illustrations, the key biblical picture of this form of discipleship comes in the New Testament church. The early church met as *oikos*, or households of faith on a common mission.

Oikos and the New Testament Church

The primary building block of Roman society was the *oikos*—a word describing a network of relationships centered around a Roman citizen, the *paterfamilias*. Every single person in that culture belonged to an *oikos*, which existed as his or her extended family or household. Your *oikos* would include people from all areas of your life:

- Family
- Friends
- Neighbors
- Relatives
- Coworkers (including slaves in the Roman culture)
- People with whom your household did business (as most businesses operated out of the home)

Essentially, your *oikos* equaled your network of current and ongoing relationships. And although we don't use that word today, we still live and relate in exactly the same way: our lives are oriented around a cluster of key relationships.

Today when we read New Testament references to the church, we tend to think of a beautiful, whitewashed, clapboard building with an elegant steeple pointing heavenward, positioned in the center of town with doors wide open on a Sunday morning. By contrast, when the first three hundred years of Christians heard the word *church*, their first thought was never of a building. Instead, the first sense of "the church" for the early Christians was their *oikos*.

The first sense of "the church" for the early Christians was their *oikos*.

This understanding helps to explain how, during its first three centuries of existence, the early church grew at a phenomenal rate. Consider estimated growth rates between the beginning of the church in AD 40 and the middle of the fourth century (see table 4).

Year	Number of Christians	Percent of Roman Empire
AD 40	1,000	0.0017%
AD 350	34 million	56.5%

》》 TABLE 4

If we average this out, we see that the number of disciples increased by about 40 percent every decade for over three centuries, which is a staggering rate of growth for just one decade, let alone thirty decades in a row!

In his tremendously helpful book *The Rise of Christianity*, sociologist Rodney Stark notes that this incredible increase took place while Christians were a persecuted minority on the margins of society, with no political power and the inability to hold public meetings. Being a Christian didn't even stop being illegal until AD 313, with some of the fiercest persecutions occurring in the years immediately prior to the legalization of Christianity under the newly converted Emperor Constantine.[33] This understanding of early Christianity should cause us, as Westerners, to stop and consider how we may have been imposing our own experience of church onto how we read the Bible.

So why was the *oikos* the perfect context for the rapid spread of Christianity throughout the known world at that time? Here are a few reasons:

- In a place where the call to discipleship is an all-in, hold-nothing-back kind of commitment, the gospel is spread and the church is most easily built among those with whom you are already doing life.

- If your *oikos* is the epicenter of your most important relationships, it is the place where you will be discipled most easily—and where you will most naturally help disciple others.

- If your *oikos* is your primary place of affinity, then church in that context will grow in number and depth in a highly organic and relational manner.

> **A disciple-making church is anchored in everyday, life-on-life, house-on-house relationships.**

- As the early Christians recognized, a disciple-making church is anchored in everyday, life-on-life, house-on-house relationships.

First Corinthians and the Oikos Church

When we read 1 Corinthians 11–14, we can see Paul coaching the early Christians on the practicalities of being an *oikos* church. We notice that Paul instructs individuals to bring and share their food so that rich and poor alike may eat and be satisfied. And Paul tells off those who are becoming drunk during Holy Communion. (Stop and think about that for a moment: How many times have you seen someone become drunk taking Communion during a worship service?) This correction makes sense only when we understand that the church was meeting in a home where there was a plentiful supply of wine. Apparently these baby disciples saw nothing wrong in overindulging!

Paul guides the members of the early church into using spiritual gifts in a manner that builds up the wider community, including those members of the *oikos* who are spiritually open but aren't yet saved. The emphasis is on a varied, responsible, yet fluid manifestation of those gifts, as led by the Holy Spirit. Paul's teaching in 1 Corinthians makes a lot more practical sense (that is, hearing different voices contribute, making room for one another, etc.) once we place it within the original Social Context–sized gathering.

Paul also demonstrates that the most important heart attitude is to reflect God's love in whatever we say and do. In a group size where we have to get along with everyone—even crazy Uncle Bob in the corner—the love commands are perhaps the most challenging (and beneficial) to live out. All of the "one another" commands throughout the New Testament are intended to be expressed and worked out within groups of twenty to seventy people.

Romans 16 and the Oikos Church

With eyes now open to the *oikos* lens through which to interpret New Testament references to the church, we will begin to spot how the Social Context was used to make disciples throughout the New Testament.

Take, for instance, the final chapter of Romans. After digging through all of the theological gems and high points in the book, some people find that chapter 16 comes across as a bit of a disappointment. We glance down the page and see nothing but a long list of greetings to long-dead people, and so we skip on to the final prayer as an apt conclusion to an amazing letter.

But let's bring our newfound appreciation of *oikos* to our reading. Viewing the text in this light will reveal many previously hidden insights into the structure of disciple making in the early church in the city of Rome.

One of the main fallacies we must overcome is the assumption that Paul is writing to a single congregation meeting in one big room all at one time. Which, of course, is complete nonsense.

In his letter, Paul is addressing multiple *oikos* expressions of church, which together make up the church in Rome. He repeatedly name-checks key people, along with their household and extended family, and recognizes many different household churches meeting in a wide variety of situations.

Professor James Dunn, perhaps the foremost scholar on the book of Romans, comments on chapter 16: "The groupings indicate at least five different house churches in Rome (v. 5, 10, 11, 14, 15)." He goes on to note "Paul's awareness that the letter would have to be read several times within the different home churches."[34]

Here's a fascinating illustration of the subversive power of *oikos* for discipleship and mission. Romans 16:15 reads, "Greet Philologus, Julia, Nereus and his sister, and Olympas and all the Lord's people who are with them." What makes these hard-to-pronounce names interesting to us today? The ones listed in verse 15 were all commonly given to slaves who were part of Caesar's palace (no, not the one in Vegas—the one that was the center of the Roman Empire!). This suggests that Paul is greeting an *oikos* church made up primarily of slaves who belong to Caesar. Dunn proposes, "Perhaps the whole group consisted of members of the imperial household, who met in 'off-hours.'"[35]

We also have a cross-reference that supports this conclusion. A few years later, Paul found himself in Rome as a prisoner awaiting trial before Caesar. During this time he wrote a letter to the church in Philippi, where he shared the following message: "All God's people here send you greetings, especially those who belong to Caesar's household" (Phil. 4:22).

Clearly there was a well-established, Jesus-following community of slaves and staff in Caesar's household—men and women, young and old, all of whom were serving the Roman Empire. How did they survive at the very center of opposition to Christ and persecution of his disciples? The clue lies in Paul's writing. He was passing on greetings from Caesar's household—literally, "Caesar's *oikos*." In other words, some of those who belonged to Caesar's *oikos* were committed to following Jesus as Lord rather than Caesar as Lord!

Such a risky, subversive stance would have been possible only through the robust, dynamic, persecution-proof relationships that develop in a Social Context–sized group, made up of twenty to seventy people who are focused around growing closer to Christ and reaching out in mission to the rest of Caesar's household. They were small enough in size to find solace, strength, and life together, and large enough to be a base for mission where the spiritually open in the imperial household could find themselves embraced and gently folded into Christian community.

This was not a unique situation. Most scholars agree that the *oikos* was the center of almost all church life until the legalization of Christianity under Emperor Constantine. (If you're an avid reader, Roger Gehring's book *House Church and Mission* will give you far more detail on this topic.)[36]

Other New Testament Examples

The apostle Paul repeatedly used the Social Context—these *oikos* households—as his primary context for both mission and discipleship. While Paul operated fruitfully in each of the Contexts, his standard process for discipleship was to identify and pour into the most spiritually open household he could find. For instance, when Paul was led to preach the gospel for the first time in Europe, the breakthrough came when Lydia and her household were converted. Her home became the base for the first church on that continent.

> **Paul's standard process for discipleship was to identify and pour into the most spiritually open household he could find.**

Further on in Acts 16, the second European church is planted in the *oikos* of the Philippian jailer. Because the gospel is allowed to flow through preexisting relational pathways, two converts—Lydia and the jailer—are rapidly multiplied into two churches.

Acts 18:7–8 tells us of a critical breakthrough in Corinth when Crispus, the leader of the local (and hostile) synagogue, comes to faith in Jesus, along with his whole household, all of which takes place in a private home. (Amusingly, we later find out that Crispus's replacement as synagogue leader, Sosthenes, also comes to faith—both are mentioned in 1 Corinthians 1.)

In Acts 10 Peter likewise uses the Social Context to extend God's kingdom through the conversion of Cornelius and his household. And at the end of Acts we see a parallel example of *oikos* growth when Paul and his companions are shipwrecked on Malta, where they share the gospel with Publius, his family, and the people in his circle of influence.

Think about what Paul did whenever he went to a new place: he found allies, worked hard, won respect, and allowed his first converts to act as gatekeepers to their *oikos* communities, where new churches would then be established. As Paul's letters indicate, it was in these *oikos* churches that the nitty-gritty of discipleship took place as individuals learned what it meant to recognize and obey the voice of Jesus within the context of Christian community.

We've seen how the early church used the Social Context frequently and to great effect. The biblical and historical evidence is powerful—but we still are left with the question of how we can do the same. After all, most of us don't live in a culture where following Jesus results in persecution, and our world is very different in many respects from the world of these early Christians. So how do we live out *oikos* principles as we seek to make and grow disciples of Jesus in our own culture and social setting?

THE SOCIAL CONTEXT FEEDS THE PUBLIC CONTEXT

In the next chapter we will look in depth at what are commonly called "missional communities." And if you are thinking ahead, you might be wondering, "Won't all this emphasis on missional communities lead people to reject public worship services and interact only in the Social Context?"

We want to be clear up front: that isn't our goal. And the key to avoiding this upshot is to have a "both/and" rather than an "either/or" mentality. As we will say many times throughout this book, the different contexts should complement, rather than compete with, each other.

However, to answer the specific question posed earlier, what we have seen is that people who join missional communities from outside of the church will, if given enough time, naturally transition over to the public worship services. Primarily this happens because they follow the relational pathways that have been forged in the missional community. They will have heard stories and reports from the weekend services, and eventually their curiosity will be stoked enough that they will ask to come along with their friends.

Recently one of our missional community leaders had this experience:

We had a Laundry of Love event at a laundromat in our community. Our families went there to pass out quarters and snacks for those who were stuck in the building doing their laundry. It was snowing that day, which created an easy opening for conversation!

One of our group members began talking with a guy about the weather and how he wished it would warm up. In response, the guy said the cold was better for his wife because she had a bad breathing condition, which meant that in summer it was hard for her to be comfortable because there was no air-conditioning in their home.

It just happened that this group member had a spare air-conditioning unit sitting in his garage, so he said he would give it to the guy in the laundromat. Phone numbers were exchanged and a time scheduled to drop off and install the air conditioner. On that morning, more conversation took place, including a great dialogue about just why this unit was being given away so generously. The recipient couple kept saying how giving away an air conditioner was "just not normal"!

Out of that came a very natural opening to invite the couple to the missional community, but they expressed more interest in the weekend worship services. The member of the group was very happy not only to share the information but also to arrange to meet them there to help settle them into the service. The couple who received the air-conditioning unit loved what they experienced and have quickly become faithful attenders in the Public Context.

Chapter Seven

MISSIONAL COMMUNITIES DEMYSTIFIED

Discipleship in the Social Context

Key Application: By choosing to plant missional communities, your church will be making numerous disciples of Jesus among those who would never otherwise come to a regular weekend service, while also enabling the church family to live out their callings and gifts in their neighborhoods and networks of relationship.

We loved our Ohio neighbors! Full of life, laughter, and generosity, great relationships formed over our first few years living in our neighborhood. Gathering spontaneously around the fire pit, sharing outdoor meals on summer evenings, helping watch one another's kids, serving one another's families when illness struck. We were genuinely blessed by their friendship.

One of the things that helped unite us was our common stage of life: raising middle and high schoolers creates a battle-scarred level of solidarity among parents! Over a drink we would laugh together at the funny moments, celebrate the successes, and commiserate over the struggles and frustrations.

As these relationships deepened, Hannah and I were sensing that our time leading our then missional community—which was for young adults— was naturally drawing to a close. A number of excellent twentysomething leaders had emerged, and they were more than ready to take it on and develop it further.

So we suggested to our neighbors that we could start gathering every few weeks to eat, connect, and seek to learn from Jesus in this crazy journey of parenting tweens and teens. We wanted the kids to be there, too, so we also talked about helping them learn about the spiritual side of life.

The initial gathering—praying for our kids as they started the new school year, after they'd had a chance to say what they were anxious about or wanted prayer for—was a great success, and the missional community (or "our faith and family group," as one of the moms named it) developed from there.

Many of the households didn't come to our church, and there was a wide range of spiritual maturity. But by creating a space where it was okay to talk about and experience spiritual issues, all sorts of movement took place. Naturally discussions about faith spilled over into other times throughout the week, and together we went on a journey toward Jesus.

For many of the parents, one of the most impacting things early on was seeing their children be invited to contribute to the community gatherings, whether in the worship, discussions, or various service opportunities. Parents heard their kids talk about spiritual matters far more openly than ever happened normally, which both encouraged and challenged the adults.

The group has found several service opportunities in the neighborhood, which both train our middle-class kids to care for those less fortunate than themselves and also help to draw in some of the fringier dads. Great conversations happen while people work to complete a common task.

More than forty-five people—adults and kids—came to the Christmas party. One of the previously quieter men shared a great insight into Christmas, and we enjoyed a wonderful sense of community together, looking forward to all that would happen among us in the year ahead.

Such stories are not unique; we hear them all the time. There is something enormously powerful about communities with a common mission that include people in various stages of their spiritual journey. And while missional communities can start up with any number of people present, we have found that the Social Context is the size in which such community formation naturally occurs.

Sadly, for many of our churches in the West, Social Context–sized gatherings are notable mostly by their absence! Like the missing piece in a jigsaw puzzle, this discipleship context tends to be overlooked by the predominant church cultures that exist today.

In the last chapter we recognized that the Social Context was a major place of disciple making both for Jesus and for the early church. Yet most churches today have very low competency in forming gatherings of this size, let alone any strategy for forming disciples. To develop a disciple-making church culture, we have to recover and restore our use of the Social Context. It is the most crucial space that exists for the formation of authentic community that is effective on mission.

Most churches and pastors operate in the Public Context fairly well but are weak in their experience and understanding of the Social Context. Even when we encounter Christian groups that seem to be the size of the Social Context—perhaps a small

> **The Social Context may be the most crucial space for the formation of authentic community that is effective on mission.**

church with thirty-five people for Sunday morning worship, or an adult Sunday school class in a larger church—they are rarely operating by the rules of the Social Context.

Such gatherings are run like miniature Public Context occasions, with everyone sitting in rows looking at the person at the front speaking to them through a microphone. While this approach may be fine in certain situations, we need to recognize that the rules that are in play will affect the outcome. Fruitful Social Context groups, which we refer to as *missional communities*, operate by a different set of rules than do Public Context gatherings.

WHAT IS A MISSIONAL COMMUNITY?

Let's define what we are talking about. To put it very simply, a missional community is a group with the following characteristics:

- Jesus at the center
- Twenty to fifty (or more) people (including children)
- A clear mission to make disciples in a specific neighborhood or network of relationships
- An intentional disciple-making culture

- An expectation of multiplication from day one (thus an emphasis on practice and team building)
- A pattern of activity that balances Up (our relationship with God), In (our relationship with one another), and Out (our relationship with the wider world)

So one way to think about missional communities is to think of your *extended family*. Imagine a healthy, vibrant extended family gathering to celebrate a holiday together. Cousins mingle, aunts and uncles chatter, grandparents dandle infants on their knees, and each person feels a sense of acceptance, belonging, and identity within the broader context.

Or think about your *front porch*, if you have one. Consider the role of the front porch in a street of homes. It is a place where you sit out with your family and interact with your neighbors and passersby. It's easy to invite someone to stop and enjoy a drink from your pitcher of lemonade, and if your "porch presence" is consistent over time, authentic community will be formed.

Your neighbors will be much more likely to accept an invitation onto your porch than an invitation to come all the way into your home—they know they can leave easily and so can test out their relationship with you in a relatively low-risk manner! If their children are with them and start acting up, they can simply make their excuses and depart.

This is an excellent picture of the environment that a growing missional community creates—a low-risk place for neighbors to enter into your community and spiritual growth, especially when compared to the intensity of a small group or the formality of a Sunday worship service.[37]

Or think of your *local coffee shop*. Bring to mind your favorite local haunt where you love to go hang out. It could be a coffee shop, café, or even your version of the bar from *Cheers*! In most cases there will be enough seating for between twenty and seventy people, which creates a Social Context space within which smaller Personal Context conversations can take place.

As a regular, you will recognize and even chat with many of the people you see in there, and at an emotional level you will feel a high degree of ownership—this is "your" coffee shop. When a larger group is in, such as when the local high school ends its day, tables are pulled together and full-on midsized community takes place.

A final image to illustrate the Social Context is a *kids' soccer team*. Think of a friendly and encouraging group that knits together the parents, siblings, and other family members of each child who is playing the sport. Whether at practice or a game, for the duration of the season a strong sense of solidarity and connection forms in such an environment.

GOALS FOR DISCIPLESHIP IN THE SOCIAL CONTEXT

The ways we can be discipled in missional communities are just about endless, but the trouble with long lists is that they become overwhelming and, therefore, functionally meaningless. In order to help our missional community leaders, we have boiled down our expectations and goals for their groups to three core things: *community*, *mission*, and *practice*.

Goal 1: Community

The defining characteristic of the Social Context is that it is your primary place of affinity—this is your wider group, your extended family, your neighborhood, your club, your gang, your team.

Anthropologists have repeatedly noted that across almost all cultures, people gain their sense of communal identity from being part of a group of between twenty and seventy people. So what is it about this size that leads to the formation of strong social bonds?

- You can reasonably expect to learn everyone's name (with all that represents), and you can expect them to learn yours as well.

- The atmosphere is very collegial. Groups like these work best when the leader is not the sole, or even primary, voice in all the conversations.

- People control how much they reveal about themselves to the whole community, while still being authentic. This makes for a low-pressure atmosphere, since each individual is able to choose their speed of entry into the community.

- We are able to make room for "Crazy Uncle Bob." Think of him this way: every extended family has a Crazy Uncle Bob (or Aunty Bobby), who at every family gathering sits in the corner grumbling, mumbling, and scaring the grandchildren! If there are thirty or forty of you, this kind of eccentric behavior is not a problem; if there are just six or eight of you sitting around the dining room table, one of whom is Crazy Uncle Bob, then your plans will be train-wrecked. Is anyone coming to mind now?

The church needs to be a community where the Crazy Uncle Bobs of the world can come and find acceptance and a pathway to healing, without their issues dominating the whole agenda of the group. The Social Context is ideal for providing this kind of environment, whereas the Personal Context simply isn't large enough to pull it off successfully.

We are able to make room for "Crazy Uncle Bob."

As we go in mission, the implicit invitation we are offering is, "Come join our community!" People have such a hunger for authentic community, and the Social Context is the best size for building a healthy yet growing expression of life together. This simple truth has been one of the secrets of the growth of the church for the past two thousand years, across all times, places, and cultures.

Remember that Jesus gave the world the right to judge us on one thing: the quality of the love we have for one another (John 13:35). We are to model a type of community that can't help but fold the lost into the love of Christ. While the anonymity of weekend services may be attractive to some for a while, eventually even the shyest individuals want to know others and be known themselves. Midsized (Social Context) missional communities usually will be the easiest way to make this happen, as they can foster relationships without demanding that newcomers go relationally "all in" from the outset.

Together these elements mean that the missional community is a place where cohesive community can be formed, a place where people can come and find a spiritual base camp for discipleship and mission.

Keep in mind that a missional community is not to be full of hype, stress, and exhausting over commitment; rather, it should be a place full of fun, life, and authenticity, where no one wants to miss out on any chance to get together! All ages gather to both give and receive. The best missional communities are incredibly attractive for both the committed member and the newcomer.

Goal 2: Mission

More and more people are discovering that the Social Context is the easiest space in which to live a shared life on mission. Both in terms of group members seeking to draw in their unchurched friends, and also from the perspective of new people entering in, this size of gathering offers the highest chance of adding people permanently to the kingdom.

Why is this?

Earlier, we explained that certain "rules" govern different sizes of gatherings. While we've never been formally taught these rules, they are our socially accepted norms. For instance, your unchurched friends

A Social Context–sized gathering offers the highest chance of adding people permanently to the kingdom.

instinctively know that they will not be expected to share private information about themselves in a room full of thirty people. Consequently, the barrier to entry at this size of gathering is pretty low, especially in comparison to a traditional small group of six to ten people.

In addition, those who are new can choose their speed of entry into the group without being perceived as rude or socially awkward. Whether they want to hang back on the edge and just observe or prefer to dive right into the heart of the conversation and action, or anything in between, their prerogative to own that choice is socially acceptable.

Inviting a friend to a group this size is easy too. To illustrate, if your unchurched neighbor is open to checking out your group, which is easier: to invite them to a backyard grill-out with twenty-five people, or to invite them to a dinner party with six people? I suspect ninety-nine times out of one hundred your friend will choose the backyard grill-out—a choice we can now explain through our understanding of the Social Context.

Encouraging people to go as a group in service and witness tends to meet with relatively little resistance in the Social Context. I can recall many times trying to do this with my small group and it being a nightmare! But in the Social Context, people intuitively will do the math and say to themselves, "There will be enough of us there to make a difference without a high risk of embarrassment, but my contribution will still count for something."

Let's say your group is made up of twelve people (which means you operate by the rules of the Personal Context) and someone suggests going to the park next Saturday at lunchtime to hand out cans of pop in the predicted sunshine. What inevitably happens is that four people suddenly discover they have work to do, three people will have child-care issues and won't make it, and three more will do the math and bail because they can see the writing on the wall for this activity. That will leave two of you and a lot of pop to take the city for Jesus!

By contrast, the no-show effect isn't as much of a problem with a Social Context–sized group. People tend to realize that, even given the genuine excuses for absence, enough people will turn out both to make the experience feel safe for them and to have a decent impact. Moreover, parents can easily bring their children to a midsized outreach effort, and while you are serving, your combined impact is readily apparent. This in turn creates a virtuous cycle: you go in mission as a midsized group and experience some encouraging fruitfulness, which in turn leads to greater motivation to go again in mission to your place of calling.

We make multiplication the expectation from day one for every group that we launch.

When you are looking outward in mission to a specific neighborhood or network of relationships, you also will be (or should be!) praying to see enough disciples being made that your group has to multiply. In our missional communities, we make multiplication the expectation from day one for every group that we launch.

Finally, the Social Context is the appropriate size for discussions about multiplication. If you have ever tried to multiply a small group, then you know how relationally costly it can be. I've done it several times and on each occasion it was heartrending for group members to see people they'd grown so close to pulled off in a different direction. If I'm honest, emotionally and relationally, multiplication can feel more like divorce.

The sociology we outline in this book explains why. In the Personal Context we share private information with one another, so at a heart level it is very painful to see those relationships break up. A small group operates by the rules of the Personal Context, which bring great value (close relationships) but also carry a weakness (that very closeness is in conflict with the impulse to multiply). By contrast, in the Social Context we share snapshots of what it would be like to be closer friends, and so when a group in the thirties or forties multiplies, it is far less costly and painful.

In appendix 3 we have included a few examples of how different mission contexts create unique ways to encounter God (Up), develop life together (In), and bless the wider world (Out).

Goal 3: Practice

Helping as many individuals as possible to discover their identity and giftedness in Christ is one of the hallmarks of a disciple-making church. But we can't just leave this goal to chance—we need to deliberately create the contexts where it can happen. Providing safe and healthy environments where people can practice their way to maturity is essential.

The Bible repeatedly tells us that spiritual gifts are given in order to build up the church into Christlikeness. However, God's gifts, while freely given, do not suddenly appear fully formed and perfected in our lives. Yet most churches have no deliberate space where character training can take place and a wide variety of spiritual gifts can be exercised.

The Social Context is an ideal size of gathering for this training and practice to take place. As we'll explain, we have found it to be the perfect size for individuals to develop, mature, and produce the fruit of what God has invested in them. And from a church's perspective, if a number of missional communities do this over a reasonable length of time, then the leadership development pipeline will have been hugely strengthened.

Let's think a little more about how missional communities work as a place of practice.

First of all, the Social Context gives people a safe place to experiment with their gifts and skills. The Public Context is too risky—simply put, a crash and burn there is tantamount to ritual humiliation! By contrast, the Personal Context often feels far too intense—for instance, if I have my first guitar, two chords, and a croaky singing voice, to inflict my new song on five friends requires lots of close eye contact and forced engagement, however awful I might be!

The Social Context gives people a safe place to experiment with their gifts and skills.

The medium size of the Social Context gives people the chance to explore and try out their spiritual gifts and life skills in a low-pressure environment, while receiving coaching and encouragement along the way. Whether someone is hosting for the first time and their living room is a complete mess, or they very falteringly share their first prophetic word, or they do a five-minute teaching but forget all their Bible references, a missional community provides a safety net where they can learn from that experience and grow into greater maturity.

Second, individuals need to be part of a wider network of believers to grow into maturity as disciples of Jesus. We can't expect to receive all our training and growth from just our nuclear spiritual family, or even from only one or two others; that's just not a wide enough network from which to draw.

Think about it this way. If discipleship is imitation, too small a gene pool will produce genetic weakness in spirituality—the equivalent of Christians with spiritual webbed feet (in going with the gospel), slowness of mind (in understanding and applying their faith), or simply poor hand-eye coordination (in handling the sword of the Spirit and the shield of faith).

Imitation works only through shared life. While there will always be a few very significant relationships that shape us, we still do best when we learn godly values by interacting with Christian people who have gifts, skills, and strengths that are different from our own.

In terms of coaching, the Social Context–sized group will contain within it a wider skill set than will be found in a small group. As a result, character development tends to be more effective and efficient, as there is a greater probability of finding someone to imitate in a particular area of life.

Likewise, each one of the APEST identities from Ephesians 4 (Apostle, Prophet, Evangelist, Shepherd, Teacher) is far more likely to be represented.

This balance of gifts will add to the life and health of the community, as well as to its fruitfulness in discipling people to maturity in Christ. (For more on our understanding of APEST, please see appendix 2.)

Our friends at St. Thomas Crookes Church in Sheffield, UK, describe their missional communities as being "large enough to dare and small enough to care." That is a brilliant summary of the value of practice that we see embedded at the core of missional communities.

If discipleship is imitation, too small a gene pool will produce genetic weakness in spirituality.

Practice with Kids

Of course, the practice of spiritual gifts is not just for adults—it is equally for children and teens. The Holy Spirit doesn't come in a junior portion for kids! The Social Context–sized group is an excellent place to give children and teens room to step forward, including as leaders.

Obviously some missional communities won't include kids. For instance, you may not want to involve children in a group that is focused on reaching college students, or impacting a specific workplace, or serving a local prison by planting a community among the prisoners.

Nevertheless, for many adults, children naturally are part of their regular life, and so they may wonder whether and how to include them in living on mission. Our friends Danielle and Paul lead a missional community focused on bringing families closer to Jesus. They gather households from within and outside the church. They have seen some tremendous life changes occur, and their group has multiplied twice. Here they describe how to help children feel like full stakeholders in the group, rather than simply tagalongs in their parents' missional community.

1. Have your children participate in the planning of your meetings, as well as the training opportunities from your church leaders. Also include them in the decision-making process of every aspect of missional life. If children are contributing, they feel like part of the community and valued members.

2. Use your children's ideas. (Be honest, sometimes they will be better ideas than yours anyway!)

3. Hear their concerns and frustrations, and solve them together. If children believe their concerns don't matter, they can feel like they don't matter. If something is frustrating to them, it should be frustrating to you. Involve them in the problem solving, just like any other valued member of your community.

4. Have children participate in the service opportunities. Children often break down social barriers more quickly than adults. Often they will lead the adults by example.

5. Have children lead the worship or teaching time. We underestimate the depth of kids' relationship with Jesus and underutilize their gifts and insights on our own spiritual journeys. Giving children the opportunity to lead also will be deeply impacting for unchurched families.

By operating in the Social Context, missional communities have the space and scope for children to be fully functioning members of the group. The next generation can be discipled in a natural and relational manner by the rest of this mini "village," and in turn they can exercise their gifts and strengthen the community as a whole.

POTENTIAL PITFALLS

As in the other contexts, discipleship in midsized missional communities can cover some—but not all—of the bases. While the Social Context tends to be the weakest area within the Western church, that doesn't make it the magic solution to any and all frustrations you've had with church life!

Healthy Social Context groups will model authenticity and acceptance, which lays the groundwork for a community that can be fruitful as people become missionaries to their shared place of calling. Put another way, if you feel that you have been welcomed and valued, then you likely will commit to the group and its mission.

The problems begin when people feel they have not been accepted. Perhaps certain subsets or cliques don't project a welcoming and gracious hospitality, or maybe the community is far more brittle and shallow than anyone dares acknowledge. Our tendency upon recognizing this truth is to circle the wagons and focus solely on life together, withdrawing from missional engagement. The thinking goes, "Once we have good community, then we will look outside ourselves."

In reality, though, this almost never happens! There will always be another relationship to fix, or person to mend, or ready excuse to focus inward upon ourselves. That's why we see missional focus and community life both as acutely necessary. They shape each other. The most magnetic communities are the ones with a common vision for mission *and* a deeply inclusive atmosphere.

Community fuels mission and mission feeds community.

A missional community needs to know exactly whom they are trying to reach with the gospel, since all other decisions will be shaped by that focus. For instance, the time you meet, the food you eat, and the type of music you play will be one thing if you are impacting young families, but something else entirely if you are reaching a residential home for older people, and your community will have an altogether different flavor if you are called to disciple motorbike riders!

Thus, in addition to knowing what you are called to do in this context, missional community leaders must realize what the group *cannot* do. It will not offer the polish or quality of the

> **Community fuels mission and mission feeds community.**

larger, more organized Public Context worship service. If people come expecting to worship in the same way they do on a Sunday morning, they will be sorely disappointed. Instead, they need to be retrained to embrace the many creative, if less "professional," opportunities to worship Jesus in the Social Context.

Likewise, members won't find the closeness of a small group that operates in the Personal Context. A missional community is not a place of raw accountability, since it includes too many people for such sharing to take place at a deep and consistent level. You can't expect to be close to everyone when you are in the Social Context—that is neither a wise nor achievable goal for a missional community. Certainly there will be some highly meaningful relationships, but the goal cannot possibly be unbridled transparency with everyone.

TWO COMMON BARRIERS

If you are reading through this material and are intrigued by the prospect of being part of a community on a shared mission, you may find yourself held back by two common barriers.

1. Your life is too busy.
2. You don't want to be an intrusive neighbor.

The best way to deal with these objections is through a mixture of intention and invitation.

1. Your Life Is Too Busy

Missional communities work only when you recognize that they are not an add-on to your already crazy life! Often church people hear this teaching and think, "How can I possibly add yet *another* thing into my already overcrowded schedule?!" This question shows that they misunderstand the nature of disciple making. God has placed you where you are today, which means *that* place is the context where you both are being discipled and are making disciples. Following are a few examples of what we mean.

What Is in Your Hands?

Instead of thinking about new things to do, take a look at what you are *already* doing. We are to serve the Lord with what he has already put into our hands. Put another way, living as a missionary is simply about being intentional in following Jesus wherever he takes us—at work or school, in our neighborhood, at the store or the gym, and so on.

To jump-start that process, look back at how you have spent the past two weeks. Look for the natural overlaps between the spiritual and the everyday—in other words, times when you can simply invite people to join you in what you are already doing, or when you can do what you were doing but with your "spiritual" spectacles on at the same time!

Eating for Jesus

A classic example of something we are already doing is the act of eating. Each of us has about twenty-one meals a week, so it's simply a matter of inviting others into one or two of those times and building from there. Choose to linger a little, sharing in food and friendship and listening both to the people you're with and to the gentle promptings of the Holy Spirit.

All of our missional communities are built around eating together. You can get started right away by copying that pattern this week. Make eating with others part of your household rhythm of living. The key to making this practice sustainable is to keep it low maintenance: when you have a group of people over to your home, remember you are not hosting a dinner party! Everyone contributes (that relaxes people), and everyone helps with the preparation and cleanup.

People who come regularly to the missional community that meets in my (Alex's) home quickly discover where all the plates, glasses, and silverware live, and they know they are expected to act as co-hosts along with us. (Newcomers rarely have the door answered by my wife or me!) Sharing duties makes hosting a missional community a much lighter weight for us. It's far less of an add-on and far more of an integration into what is already there in our lives.

We would also encourage you to have fun! Community life is meant to be enjoyable, not drab or always serious. When we bought a Labrador puppy, Molly's mischief and energy became fully part of our missional community. The group played their part in training her, and she is part of our life together. The everyday stuff of our family life (a new pet) is a context where discipleship and community can take place without adding anything extra to our schedule.

Share Adventure

The *oikos* in the New Testament was a center of activity and interest. Everyone shared a common mission, which no doubt created a spirit of adventure and camaraderie. As a missional community, find ways to share in new, interesting, or challenging tasks.

For instance, a few years ago my wife, Hannah, and I were making plans to take our boys to Peru, to visit and serve alongside some close friends who are planting churches through missional communities. We were already committed to the trip and had the time blocked out on our calendars. It was therefore no great burden to open the trip up to our missional community, which at that time was one for young adults. Not only was it a valuable way to invest in them, but it also enriched our experience and simply added to the fun and interest for our children.

Be Vulnerable

A couple of years ago I had a serious illness and struggled with the temptation to simply withdraw from the community. However, we went the other way, inviting and welcoming our friends and neighbors to walk alongside us through it all. That decision served to strengthen and deepen our friendship with those in our missional community, and all the support we received was a very practical blessing to my family.

Life together is about giving and receiving. Though it sounds somewhat counterintuitive, by choosing to be vulnerable, we will discover that the pressures on our time actually lessen.

● ● ●

Don't forget that living in community is not all fun and games. Sometimes it's just hard work to follow Jesus. There will be times and seasons when our reserves are depleted, and sometimes we just have to take it on the chin and keep on persevering. We receive the kingdom of God by grace, but it costs us absolutely everything. We must learn to be intentional in using the time and opportunities in our lives.

> **We receive the kingdom of God by grace, but it costs us absolutely everything.**

2. You Don't Want to Be an Intrusive Neighbor

Hopefully you are not one of "those" neighbors who just steamrolls through all relational boundaries with an alarming lack of sensitivity and self-awareness! For each of us it is vital to develop a very invitational attitude toward our colleagues and neighbors. Here are several ways we can do this:

- *Give permission.* Encourage those whom you are discipling (whether or not they view themselves as Christians) to share in your life. Always try to find a way to say yes, to let them call on you and rely on you.

- *Share what you own.* "Come use our grill / play with our dog / borrow the lawn mower," and so on. Be generous with your time, energy, and resources. And then accept the reciprocal gestures.

- *"Hey, just call in!"* Don't pull up the drawbridge when you are at home! Encourage and welcome unexpected knocks on the door so that people always feel that you are approachable. In the workplace this attitude is important as well, especially if you lead others—try out an "open door" policy on your colleagues. Work is a great place to develop more confidence in these skills, as you naturally have multiple interactions there during the day.

- *Start doing it to them!* While knocking on your neighbor's door at 1:00 a.m. probably isn't a smart idea, there are lots of times when you can appropriately connect with friends and neighbors. Try doing the quick, "We were just passing and thought we'd say 'Hi!'" and then leave before you've massively derailed their plans. Observe how people respond to that—it can open up some great conversations.

- *Join in when you're invited.* Anytime you're invited to a social event among the people you are trying to reach, say yes and be fully present when you are there!

> **Don't pull up the drawbridge when you are at home!**

GROWING THE CHURCH

We hope that these ideas will fuel your imagination and help you rediscover the power of groups of twenty to seventy people. Using the Social Context to develop missional communities is vital for the church to grow in our increasingly post-Christian culture.

Some of your unchurched neighbors and colleagues may accept an invitation to come with you to a Public Context service, and if that is the case, make the most of it. However, many of your friends are never going to turn up on a Sunday morning, no matter how contemporary the worship or insightful the preaching. Whether or not you think that is fair is beside the point—they aren't coming, so we need to have more than just one strategy for drawing people to Christ.

Again, we want to be clear that we definitely like the idea of people coming to Public Context worship services so that they receive all the rich benefits of that space. As explained in chapters 3 and 4, certain aspects of discipleship are most readily appropriated in that place. However, too many churches act as if everyone is going to come to Christ through the Public Context, when self-evidently that is not the case in a post-Christian culture.

Our friend Alan Hirsch reckons that only around 40 percent of the population would consider coming to a traditional church service, which means that 60 percent of people require a different sort of approach. Most churches focus all their energies on the 40 percent, so instead of fighting them, how about investing more in a "blue ocean" strategy for discipling the 60 percent?

Make this personal for you right now. Write down the name of a friend who is in the 60 percent—in other words, they are not a Christian and almost certainly would not come with you to a church service this coming weekend. Yet you love them and long to see them walking as a committed disciple of Jesus.

We need to work out how to be missionaries in our culture who make disciples. For too long we as the church have focused almost solely on reaching those who will come to us, at a time and place of our choosing. This places the burden of change, of needing to shift cultures to fit into the little world we have created, entirely on those we are seeking to reach. No wonder the Western church is struggling!

Even a passing glimpse at the New Testament reveals that the current strategy for discipleship is not the primary commission Jesus has given us. He is clear: we are to go *out* into the world, meeting people on their turf, representing Jesus in that environment, working out what good news would look like in that place, and forming expressions of church that are fully faithful to the gospel yet also fully incarnated into that particular neighborhood or network of relationships.

Success, when envisioned this way, becomes less about the number of seats filled in our services or the amount of money given (although we still count those things) and far more about the number of people involved in discipling relationships. We look for signs and indicators of people maturing as disciples through the stories that are told, the good fruit in their lives, the growth in community, and the increasing ability of those individuals to in turn go and make more disciples. In other words, we foster a culture of multiplication rather than addition.

Of course, the drawback to this approach is that it's a slower burn process, since many of these friends are much farther back spiritually. However, in the long run, it is a much wiser strategy, since by forming Jesus-centered communities on a common mission, you are far more likely to make disciples of a vast swath of people who otherwise never would be reached and transformed.

FINAL THOUGHTS

Oikos—the extended household on a common mission—is the bedrock of most societies and was the structural center of the New Testament church. Don't forget it was a church that was heavily persecuted, yet it was able not only to survive but to grow by 40 percent for each of over thirty decades.

A Social Context–sized *oikos*, or missional community, is both a biblical and a sociological model. It makes great sense for churches and individuals who are committed to making disciples who make disciples, and it will help build a multiplying, decentralized missional culture.

> A Social Context–sized *oikos*, or missional community, is both a biblical and a sociological model.

We'll close this chapter with the story of one missional community (in this church they are called GoCommunities, or GoCos for short) with an amazing vision. It was birthed out of the experience of one woman who walked alongside a number of family members who fought cancer. Out of her tenacity and refusal to give the last word to the enemy, the group was born.

There's just something about cancer that bonds people for life. It doesn't matter what kind of cancer or what the outcome. We all have stories. We have wounds and scars. We have wins. We have losses. Above all, together, we find incredible hope and strength.

The Cancer Warriors GoCo is a group who are passionate about serving and encouraging cancer patients and their families. We've all had experience battling all types of cancer, either personally or alongside our own close family members and friends. We know firsthand the spiritual, emotional, and physical battle that takes place when facing cancer and it's a time in your life when you run either toward or away from God. Cancer Warriors GoCo is ready and willing to serve in Jesus' name just as we were served, and to give back to others like so many who stood by and supported us during each of our cancer stories.

Our group meets twice a month and we usually serve together as a large group at least one other time a month. We are happy to serve as needed to take care of people's practical needs and love to develop relationships with patients and their families. We serve both as a large group and individually, as we aim to use our own gifts and passions in serving others. We have people who can help drive patients to their appointments through the American Cancer Society's Road to Recovery Program. We have people in the group who are talented hairstylists willing to help patients with wigs. We have a photographer who has a passion to serve by capturing on film the stories of families and individuals we serve. The list goes on! It's a win-win anytime we can use our God-given gifts and talents for the benefit of the patients and families we feel called to serve.

We also pray for those with cancer, for Jesus' healing, and also for their family and friends. Sometimes that involves walking with people to the end of their lives, but we want to see more and more people healed and set free!

As a large group, together we can help individuals with anything from cards and visits to household needs and meals. We also love connecting with other GoCos to help serve! Leveraging other GoCos to help just multiplies the practical value and the kingdom impact that can be made.

GETTING STARTED

1. (For church leaders:) With your key leaders, think through how you can wisely release the first generation of missional community leaders. Brainstorm what you don't know how to do—and who you can learn from in order to maximize your fruitfulness.

2. In your context, what about your existing community life is rich and abundant, and what requires some challenge and development? Take time to apply these questions to your own life as well!

3. How can you raise up the value of living on a common mission? Are you personally being called to pioneer in this realm? What is your first "next step"?

4. How might making space for everyone to practice their spiritual gifts end up tangibly enhancing your church's leadership pipeline? What can you do to be an equipper and releaser of others?

ADDITIONAL RESOURCES FOR THE SOCIAL CONTEXT

Breen, Mike, and Alex Absalom. *Launching Missional Communities: A Field Guide.* Pawleys Island, SC: 3DM, 2010.

Frost, Michael, and Alan Hirsch. *The Shaping of Things to Come: Innovation and Mission for the 21st-Century Church,* rev. ed. Grand Rapids: Baker Books, 2013.

Halter, Hugh, and Matt Smay. *The Tangible Kingdom: Creating Incarnational Community; The Posture and Practices of Ancient Church Now.* San Francisco: Jossey-Bass, 2008.

McNeal, Reggie. *Missional Communities: The Rise of the Post-Congregational Church.* San Francisco: Jossey-Bass, 2011.

Vanderstelt, Jeff. *Saturate: Being Disciples of Jesus in the Everyday Stuff of Life.* Wheaton, IL: Crossway, 2015.

Chapter Eight

WHAT YOU KNOW ABOUT SMALL GROUPS COULD BE WRONG

Understanding the Personal Context

Key Principle: In the Personal Context, a group of between four and twelve people (or more), discipleship focuses on closeness, support, and challenge.

PERSONAL

It took us (Bobby and some leaders in his church) an unusual amount of time to persuade Mandy and Anyon to get into a small group, our weekly gathering of four to twelve people (or more). I am not sure why, but they were "small group resistant." Every Sunday we tell people that there are parts of the Christian life envisioned in the Bible that can be lived out in a church context only if we are involved in personal relationships with each other, outside Sunday gatherings, in our discipling communities.[38] Sunday is not enough if we aim for the fellowship and personal support described in the Bible.

Then an unexpected tragedy hit.

Mandy gave birth to her first baby, and three days later the child died.

In their grief, this couple finally allowed people to invest in them and love them personally. Because of the relationships that were built, Mandy and Anyon agreed to get into a group. Slowly, and for the first time, they began to form friendships inside our church community. The group meetings became more and more important to them every week.

They looked into the Bible with us and shared their lives. Mandy started to meet outside the weekly gatherings with the other women. Phone conversations became regular occurrences where sharing flourished. When Mandy and Anyon told the group they were expecting another baby, everyone celebrated together, but anxiety became Mandy's companion. Would this baby also die?

The small group was there for them. Several of the older women had enough life experience to guide Mandy through the horror of her loss, while trusting God with the future. Mandy said she could *never* have done it alone.

On the anniversary of their first baby's death, Mandy and Anyon experienced what they described was one of the most memorable outpourings of love they had ever experienced. The group leaders asked them to meet at the church building instead of the usual home setting that night. They had a picnic and Bible study outside on the church grounds.

When the meeting time ended, a leader asked Mandy and Anyon to join the others near a freshly cut hole in the ground. A man in the group pulled his pickup truck to the spot and the men unloaded a tree. Then the group joined together and put the tree in the ground, dedicating it to their lost child. There were no dry eyes that night. They said that they could never thank everyone enough for the support. Every week, coming to church, they saw the tree and it helped them grow through their grief. These people had become their trusted friends.

That night I wondered, what would have happened if they had been alone, unconnected to our small group? Who would have supported them and helped them to trust and follow Jesus through these challenging events?

THE PERSONAL CONTEXT

The Personal Context is the place where we experience relational closeness, support, and challenge. We in the Western church are relationally starved. Because our lives are so busy, we lack the time to form deep relationships. This hunger for relationships has propelled a small group revolution over the last forty years.

If the Social Context is comparable to an extended household, then the Personal Context is more like a large, single family unit or a gathering of friends for a dinner party. Typically it will be a group of between four and twelve people, or more. Once the group becomes sixteen, seventeen, or eighteen people, the dynamics start to significantly change. In a context of four to twelve, we feel comfortable sharing personal and relational information. It's a natural size for having people just "come on over," and it is ideal for sharing personal thoughts and feelings about our lives and relationships.

Usually in this context we stand between 18 inches and 4 feet apart. We are close enough to really see and know each other: our strong points, weak spots, warts, wrinkles, and all! The word commonly used to describe these relationships is *fellowship*. In the Bible, fellowship is a personal bond of relationship based on our shared life grounded in Jesus.

In a group this size, each individual can develop close friendships and let down their guard. The trust that can be established at this level is significant, especially when the group spends extended time together. Spending time together eventually leads to shared common experiences and memories. The Personal Context tends to promote relational closeness and bonding more than the Social Context does because more time is available to develop deep relationships with the others in the group. But it is not as close as some would like. (More on that below.)

We are close enough to really see and know each other: our strong points, weak spots, warts, wrinkles, and all!

And this is the real beauty of small groups—we have time to focus on building these relationships. The Personal Context is characterized by a relational focus where we share our lives, and God uses that focus to enable us to make disciples. This context also gives us an opportunity to know people who may be quite different from us in background, personality, gifts, and skills. This diversity differentiates the Personal Context from the next smaller level, the Transparent Context, where even closer and more intimate relationships are formed.

Jesus in the Personal Context

Jesus spent much of his time in the Personal Context. Jim Putman leads a large church based on small groups, and he always says to me (and others), "I believe in and focus on small groups, because that is the primary way that Jesus made disciples." He makes a good point.

At my church we repeatedly talk about the importance of small groups for discipleship, following Jesus' example. Neal McBride also describes how Jesus ministered in the context of a small group, and we find his summary very helpful (with a few modifications).[39]

McBride points out that Jesus focused his ministry around a small group (Matt. 4:18–22; Luke 6:13). Jesus didn't personally require the companionship of the Twelve, but this group of men was the focus of his ministry and relational efforts. The relationships in the group of Twelve were not the only discipling relationships Jesus had, but he did concentrate most of his time, attention, and energy on nurturing this small group.

Jesus focused on the small group more than the public group gatherings. Jesus ministered in all of the different contexts we are looking at in this book, but he prioritized his time with the small group. Jesus proclaimed the kingdom to large crowds and met with groups of twenty to seventy people in homes, but he spent considerable time with his special group of twelve. Each of these forms of ministry was crucial to his mission. Yet the group of twelve received Jesus' best in terms of his time, energy, and attention. Jesus was with his disciples all the time, as they walked along the road and as they met in different homes and different contexts. As Jesus' crucifixion drew closer, he spent more and more time with his social group and small group, and less time with the great crowds who sought him out.

Jesus' method of discipleship focused on relationships, not organization. Jesus invited people, first and foremost, into relationships. The real-life context of these relationships—including the dynamics of selfishness (James and John), impulsive actions (Peter), and misunderstanding (the Twelve)—was the context out of which Jesus made disciples. He easily could have remained aloof from any relationships that entangled and inconvenienced him with human needs and suffering. Yet as a practical demonstration of the gospel, he chose to spend time with people—caring, healing, listening, forgiving, teaching, celebrating, coaching.

Jesus used the small group context to teach and model. Jesus modeled the life of the kingdom for his disciples in a small group exactly the way that God taught the Israelites to lead their children in Deuteronomy 6. It was not an educational or academically focused experience; the small group members just did life with him wherever he went. The small group of twelve was like a large nuclear family or tight-knit group of friends in which Jesus taught them about his kingdom using a life-on-life model.

Jesus used the small group as his forum for leadership development. Jesus called the future leaders of the church into a small group relationship with himself. He gave his life to these men as he trained and discipled them and then entrusted the future of his whole ministry to them. Jesus gave both this relational model and his message of salvation that the world would come to believe.

It was with the Twelve that Jesus taught his most important lessons:

- What true greatness means (Mark 9:35)
- What love looks like (John 13:1–38)
- How to spread the gospel in word and deed (Luke 10; Mark 9)

Moreover, many of the high points in Jesus' life and ministry occurred exclusively with the Twelve:

- When the crowds didn't understand a parable, he shared the meaning with his disciples (Mark 4:34).
- He revealed his power to the Twelve when he calmed the wind and the waves (Matt. 8:23–27).
- After he fed the five thousand, the Twelve were the only ones left (John 6:67).
- He predicted his arrest and death to the Twelve (Matt. 20:17–19).
- He shared private information with the Twelve (John 13–17).
- He ate his Last Supper with the Twelve (Matt. 26:20).
- He sent out the Twelve and debriefed with them only (Luke 9:1–11).
- After the resurrection, he appeared specifically to the Twelve before appearing to others (Luke 24:30–36; 1 Cor. 15:5).

The Personal Context is the perfect environment for asking questions and applying the transformative power of the gospel to individual life.

Clearly, discipleship in the Personal Context is vital for those who want to follow Jesus and make disciples like Jesus did. In personal relationships that are grounded in a shared desire to grow as disciples, we should expect to have experiences similar to those of Jesus and his disciples. The Personal Context is the perfect environment for asking questions, watching as our leaders show us the way, and applying the transformative power of the gospel to individual life. For example, in a small group you can ask questions like these:

- What kind of life is pleasing to God?
- What does it mean to love like Jesus?
- How do we spread the gospel in word and deed?
- What does it mean to live a holy life?
- What does God want us to do with our money?

The answers to these questions aren't simple. Discipleship is about more than just learning facts and repeating information. It's about learning to apply the gospel to our lives and, along with others, working out the implications of Jesus' teachings at a personal, practical level.

Other Bible Examples

The Personal Context appears elsewhere in the Bible as well. For example, it was used in the Old Testament by the Israelites to resolve personal disputes. Soon after Moses led the people out of Egypt, he reached his leadership capacity. Seeing that he was in over his head, Moses' father-in-law, Jethro, pointed out the problem: Moses was trying to do it all by himself (Exodus 18). Moses had taken all the responsibility for the nation upon himself by judging every dispute, so Jethro advised him to place leaders over the people to help out. Following Jethro's suggestion, Moses divided the nation into a pyramid of group sizes, the smallest of which consisted of ten men. These small groups were vital units, and each group of ten had its own leader.

As we mentioned in a previous chapter, some of the house gatherings in the New Testament church may have been of the Personal Context size. While most of them fit the Social Context *oikos* size, some Bible passages seem to refer to gatherings that equate more directly to our experience of small group life. In Acts 5:42 and 20:20, for example, we read that the apostles taught publicly and also from house to house. These texts indicate that meetings in homes were fairly common at that time.

Other contexts may fit indirectly into this size of gathering as well. For example, in James 5:13–18 we see the elders gathering with people for confession, anointing with oil, and healing. Likely this text reflects occasions when a smaller gathering of people joined together within a larger social, or *oikos*, context.

SMALL GROUPS AND DISCIPLESHIP TODAY

Small groups are not a new idea. Many churches have small groups or have turned their traditional Sunday school classes into small groups. This revolution has been one of the hallmarks of North American evangelicalism over the last forty years. Our busy lives, where we are consumed with work and play, lead us to crave meaningful relationships and deeper fellowship with others.

When churches develop small groups, they often do so in an attempt to meet this need for personal relationships. Churches have learned that if they don't meet this need, people will look elsewhere. Some churches set out a handful of purposes or goals for their small group ministry, such as the following:

- Fellowship
- Bible study
- Prayer
- Relational support

Each of these objectives is good and even biblical. But one thing, perhaps the most crucial thing for the Personal Context, is missing. Think of it this way: Do any of these objectives describe Jesus' prime objective? What was his main goal when he gathered and ministered to his own twelve disciples?

We believe that muddled thinking on this point is the root cause behind much of the disillusionment people have with small groups today. Many people and churches have tried small groups but found them lacking. Officially, leaders know that their people need small groups; they just don't seem to "work" the way we want them to.

Many people and churches have tried small groups but found them lacking.

To be clear, we are not saying we have the solution to all small group problems. But we believe that Jesus and the New Testament show us the foundational goal around which every small group needs to be organized: discipleship.

So what does this mean? When Jesus asked the men who became his disciples to join him, he did not say it was for fellowship, although fellowship was a key aspect of their time together. When Jesus invited them to join him, he did not say it was for Bible study, although Bible study was a part of it. He did not say it was for prayer, even though they prayed together. And he did not ask them to come together for mutual relational support, though each one inevitably received support from the group.

Jesus invited these twelve men into his small group so they could become disciples who in turn would make more disciples.

Jesus invited these twelve men into his small group so they could become disciples who in turn would make more disciples.

Mark 1:17 provides a framework for Jesus' ministry in the Personal Context. "And Jesus said to them, 'Follow me, and I will make you become fishers of men'" (Mark 1:17 ESV). He invited his disciples into personal relationships so that they could follow him, be taught and changed by him, and then join his mission of making disciples. I believe this verse can be a helpful way to unpack our definition of a disciple. It's easy to reference and memorize, and we use it in our church and in the Relational Discipleship Network, which is a network of likeminded churches committed to discipleship.[40]

Mark 1:17 describes why Jesus called the Twelve together and becomes a framework for the three key elements of discipleship:

1. "Following" Jesus

2. Being changed by Jesus through the Holy Spirit ("I will make you . . .")

3. Committing to the mission of Christ ("fishers of men")

These three elements lead to the following definition of a disciple (referred to earlier):

A disciple is following Jesus, is being changed by Jesus, and is committed to the mission of Jesus.

I (Bobby) come back to this definition whenever I talk about disciples. If people are *following* Jesus, are being *changed* by Jesus, and are *committed* to the *mission* of Jesus, then they are biblical disciples. And I would add that this kind of clarity is essential when you start a small group ministry. The fundamental question we need to ask is, Why are we having small groups? And the answer for Jesus, in calling the Twelve together, was so that he could make disciples who made disciples.

A related question to keep in mind in the Personal Context is the discipleship question: How is our small group going to help people follow Jesus, be changed by him, and commit to his mission?

We also must consider the leadership question: Who will lead our groups? The objective of anyone leading a small group, if Jesus is our example, is to make disciples of Jesus who make disciples. Leaders are responsible for discipling those in their small group. So, like Jesus, then, they will implement practices like fellowship, Bible study, prayer, and mutual support, all with the goal of developing a person who is equipped and ready to disciple others.

Small Groups as Part of a Church's Discipleship System

If small groups are the primary context for personal discipleship, you will need an infrastructure to support this goal or the system will fall apart. Small group leaders can become disciple makers only if they too are being discipled. The whole small group system (and the whole church for that matter) will need to be built explicitly around the biblical mission of discipleship in order to work effectively. While we won't go into detail here on how to do this, you may want to look at the resources recommended at the end of chapter 9.

When your small groups are structured for discipleship, the following system is typically in place:

Small group leaders can become disciple makers only if they too are being discipled.

- The small group leader is responsible for making sure that everyone in the group is being appropriately discipled to their point of willingness.

- The small group leader is *discipling* an apprentice leader who is preparing to make disciples (typically in a Transparent Context).

- The small group leader is also *being discipled* by a coach or another leader in a relational context (typically in a Transparent Context).

For such a system to work in a local church, the entire church community must support it, particularly the lead minister or pastor and all of the other church leaders. In his book *The Tipping Point*, Malcolm Gladwell writes, "If you want to bring fundamental change to people's lives and behavior, a change that will persist and influence others, you need to create a community around them where those new beliefs could be practiced, expressed, and nurtured."[41]

This side of heaven, we won't experience a perfect small group, but that shouldn't keep us from trying. And our best chance of experiencing a healthy group life is by following Jesus' method for small groups. Patterning our efforts after Jesus' example makes all the difference when it comes to the longevity of our groups. If we establish a healthy structure of relationships to support disciples in a diverse community, we set them up well for lifelong discipleship.

An example of this principle can be found in the contrast between John Wesley's and George Whitefield's ministries of evangelism in the eighteenth century. These two men cared deeply for the lost and prayed that as many people as possible would come to know God. Only one of them chose to organize and structure his ministry for the long haul of discipleship, while the other focused on converting the masses. Their emphases were different, and certainly, anytime a person expresses faith, heaven rejoices! But some efforts last beyond the work of the individual. While efforts focused on conversion are necessary, they are just the beginning; discipleship is focused on the whole journey, from *before a person comes to faith* to *conversion* and to *a life of imitating Jesus until death*. Small groups are a great way to help people with each step in that journey.

George Whitefield preached an estimated eighteen thousand sermons, reaching about ten million people in his lifetime through field preaching during the First Great Awakening (1730s–40s).[42] He was friends with Wesley and convinced him to take his theological training out of the church and into the courtyard. Wesley preached an estimated forty thousand sermons in his lifetime, traveling 250,000 miles on horseback.[43] He organized new converts into classes of twelve people.[44] These groups met every week and asked each other about their walk with God. This structure, combined with the specific methods for discipling in small groups, caused the members of his movement to be labeled "Methodists." They were very methodical in planning for continued growth in Christ. And the fruit of that movement has lasted for generations. We have heard it said that Whitefield later lamented that his ministry was not as good as Wesley's because he did not create as many disciples!

That said, the structure of personal relationships alone will not accomplish God's work of discipleship. Simply placing ourselves in a small group does not automatically make us disciples. Indeed, sociology can never supplant the work of the Spirit when it comes to discipleship. The structure simply creates the context for growth to occur—in this case, for personal spiritual training, coaching, support, and multiplication to take place. The structure of the Personal Context can position us to become more devout disciples and disciple makers.

> **Sociology can never supplant the work of the Spirit when it comes to discipleship.**

Our part, as disciples, is to show up, be consistent, and open our hearts to the Spirit of God living inside of us. God's part is to work within us and guide the process. In all contexts, discipleship is guided by God as we align ourselves with his will.

GOALS FOR DISCIPLESHIP IN THE PERSONAL CONTEXT

There are so many ways we can be discipled in small group settings, and different models and structures may have different functions within a church. And different ministries of a church may have different approaches to small groups. But we believe three goals are common to all discipleship that occurs in the Personal Context: *closeness*, *support*, and *challenge*.

Goal 1: Closeness

Authentic friendships develop in this context. God reveals himself in various ways, and one way he does that is through other people. This happened uniquely through the person of Jesus Christ, and Jesus now pours out his gifts and his blessings upon us as the corporate body of Christ. Living in obedience to him, we become the hands, feet, and voice of Christ for those with whom we are in community. As the Scripture says, we must "encourage one another daily" (Heb. 3:13).

In the opening chapter of Romans, Paul is writing to a church he has never visited. He wants to strengthen them, but that will require his physical presence: "I long to see you so that I may impart to you some spiritual gift to make you strong—that is, that you and I may be mutually encouraged by each other's faith" (1:11–12). This passage tells us that Paul himself needed encouragement in his faith, even as an apostle of God. But we also learn that someone else's faith, when experienced in person—in physical proximity—has great power. This is different from listening to a podcast, watching church online, or even reading the Bible in solitude. Certainly these practices can be valuable, but we also need spiritual friendship with real, flesh-and-blood human beings in order to follow Jesus and experience the power of the Holy Spirit.

Consequently, we must seek to create a church culture that cultivates these types of spiritual friendships. We have a unique opportunity, "in a warped and crooked generation . . . [to] shine among them like stars in the sky" (Phil. 2:15).

For example, there is an increasing number of single people in our country and in our churches. The church will need to ask some hard questions. Foremost among them is, How does the radical love of Christ in us shape our community lifestyle in groups? Are we willing to commit to family style relationships that include a growing number of singles as our brothers and sisters in Christ? We will need to give careful thought, for example, to how we can offer spiritual friendship to those struggling with the loneliness of never being married or of being divorced or of being homosexual while seeking to trust and follow Jesus in a celibate lifestyle.

I bring up such a controversial issue because so many singles are struggling to live in a way that is consistent with the call to follow Jesus;

they need the encouragement and closeness of other faithful Christians in a small group. The old idea, in many places, that a small group is just a group of friends at a similar stage of life will not be sufficient. We know from the testimony of individuals like Wesley Hill (a celibate gay Christian leader) and others that continued growth in Christian discipleship is possible only with significant close personal relationships in a spiritual community. (See the blog *SpiritualFriendship.org*.) Rosaria Butterfield, a former high profile leader in an LGBT community, poignantly describes the essential role that close Christ-centered relationships played in her conversion and subsequent growth as a disciple of Jesus.[45]

As we seek to follow Jesus, we need friends to help us resist the world. Sharing life with others in a small group develops a depth and closeness that builds over time as we navigate the joys and sorrows of life together.

Goal 2: Support

To face the difficult challenges of life as disciples of Jesus, each one of us not only needs closeness; we need personal support—that's the way God designed us. When we live out our lives in the tight, close-knit community of the Personal Context, we find real help for dealing with personal issues. Simply having a support net with which we share our hopes, fears, and concerns gives us the safety to risk, to dream, and to grow.

The support we offer each other comes through authentic and consistent interactions in various contexts. Through these close relationships we can know one another well enough to speak into each other's lives, pray for specific needs, and enjoy God together. That is the kind of community we are looking for, and it is a major way God teaches us to listen well to his voice as he disciples us.

Having a support net with which we share our hopes, fears, and concerns gives us the safety to risk, to dream, and to grow.

The Personal Context fosters this sense of community particularly well, because it is the place where we share private information. By choosing to mutually reveal personal thoughts and feelings, we build rapport with one another and come to feel comfortable sharing our everyday ups and downs, learning and growing together.

As we recognize that our small group is a supportive place, we begin to feel confident revealing what is actually going on inside ourselves. This depth of sharing simply isn't possible in the larger contexts. (After all, who wants to listen to thirty individual prayer requests, let alone try to remember them?) The Personal Context is the ideal place to experience the joy of giving and receiving Jesus-honoring support.

Goal 3: Challenge

Within a place where we experience closeness and support, we also need a healthy dose of challenge! Following Jesus is not always easy or comfortable, and there are times when each of us needs to be called to account for our words or deeds. While a small group may not be the best place to address highly sensitive issues, a lot of situations *can* be confessed and dealt with constructively in the Personal Context.

Maybe you're discussing a particular topic from the Bible and being honest about where you personally are struggling to trust and follow Jesus. In a kind and loving way, your small group can help you process what Jesus is saying to you and what you are going to do in response. Here are the sorts of questions you might ask:

- Are you seeing your circumstances clearly and accurately?
- Are you being too hard, or too soft, on yourself?
- Why have you been responding in less than ideal ways up to now?
- How can others around you help you gain a true perspective on yourself and this situation?
- How can you plan to live differently in the week ahead?
- What practical disciplines or next steps can you implement to give yourself the best chance of success?
- Who can help you follow through on your commitment?
- What will you do if you stumble along the way and mess up again?
- How will we as a group know whether you have truly changed?

These are not meant to be legalistic rules to follow but rather are thoughtful questions to open up healthy and profitable dialogue within the environment of a safe and supportive small group.

To receive this type of challenge is a gift, and to bring it into the life of another is a tremendous privilege. It is through honest sharing and loving accountability that we grow in our walk with Jesus, and in this way small groups truly bring impetus to our journey of discipleship.

LIFE IN CLOSE COMMUNITY

Discipleship in the Personal Context is life in close community with trusted friends. In our church, many have personally experienced the transformative power of God through these relationships and have witnessed how God has worked in others' lives, even when they couldn't see it at first. Having established these relationships, we are better prepared to handle the unexpected challenges of life, such as losing a child, facing the loneliness of the single adult life, and other challenges; God works through these relationships for our good. Throughout church history, the Personal Context has proven effective for disciple making. The contrast between John Wesley's and George Whitefield's ministries offers an example on a large scale of the fruitful effect of structured discipleship within small groups.

Most important, though, the life of Christ was centered upon just twelve men. He invested most of his time, effort, and teaching into this ragtag group of guys, but this was his choice, his master plan. As disciple makers, we must look to Jesus, the Great Disciple-Maker, for not only *what* he taught but *how* he taught it. The Personal Context is a critical part of our growth as disciples.

Chapter Nine

CREATING A GREAT SMALL GROUP

Discipleship in the Personal Context

Key Application: Provide opportunities for personal discipleship through small groups and similar gatherings like a reformatted Sunday school class.

PERSONAL

Gigi first showed up on a Sunday morning. She was a little late for the church service and Cindy, my (Bobby's) wife, helped her get her daughter to the nursery. It was quickly apparent that this single mom felt harried. But she was very grateful for my wife's help.

Before long Gigi was a regular on Sunday mornings. She had a good, strong Christian heritage, but she had fallen out of the habit of regular Bible study and had lost all of her close church relationships. We later found out that she was a successful business leader (the founder of Gigi's Cupcakes, a national chain) and led a very busy life! We convinced Gigi that she needed a small group if she wished to grow as a disciple of Jesus, and she finally gave in. She told us it had been over ten years since she'd been in a Bible study or met with someone in a close discipling relationship.

And then, as we expected it would, "it" happened. Slowly and almost imperceptibly at first, over time the relationships in our small group changed her life. I was invited in one day to watch some video testimonies for a building campaign, and I saw Gigi on camera. Her story stunned me. I remembered her as someone who reluctantly joined our small group, and yet here, to the whole church, she was singing the praises of small groups! She shared how the Bible study, the friendships, and especially the discipleship environment had forever changed her life.

In the last chapter we looked at some of the biblical basis for engaging in discipleship in the Personal Context, especially in the life of Jesus. And we saw how this context typically manifests itself as a small group ministry in your church. We learned the three key outcomes for this context: closeness, support, and challenge. While the biblical account of Jesus with his twelve disciples is a great ideal for us to study, what does a healthy small group look like in our day? How does discipleship work effectively in the Personal Context today?

DISCIPLESHIP IN THE PERSONAL CONTEXT

In the Personal Context, you can let your guard down and reveal more of yourself to a small group of people. This level of closeness is easier to attain in a small group than in a large group because the rules, so to speak, are different.

The expectations have changed because the context has changed.

One rule is fixed for many small groups, and it is often considered nonnegotiable. What people share in the group is to remain private. Not everyone will feel safe unless your ground rules include practices or confidentiality clauses like this. While the leader of the group is responsible for making this rule clear to the entire group, participants can always implement this principle too.

What people share in the group is to remain private.

Why is privacy such a concern? Because privacy is a key characteristic—and expectation—of the relationships we have in this context. Just as sharing too much of one's life can violate social norms in the Public Context, so sharing too little can hinder discipleship at the small group level. While the details disclosed here tend to be less intimate than those shared in the Transparent Context (as we will see below), the Personal Context is the place for close relationships and open sharing of our everyday struggles and joys. That doesn't make it appropriate to divulge every detail, but it's important to be appropriately open with your group about real struggles and victories. To whom else will you open up? And thinking beyond what you can receive from the group, recognize that the small group context is a place where you can give life to others, through your words, prayers, and actions, as you are filled with the Spirit of life (Rom. 8:2).

So what does small group discipleship look like today? Do people find a group in the church and join it? Or does someone ask people to be their disciples and follow them around like Jesus asked his disciples to do? Is it something only pastors do? If not, how do regular church members make disciples? And how can we all learn to listen well to God in this context?

Setting the Key Expectations

While there will be variation, we have found the following principles to be helpful. Many people have given up on small groups in churches because of bad experiences, so we want to be thoughtful.

First, never forget that it's about discipleship. We touched on this principle in the last chapter, but we'll repeat it again here. The purpose of these gatherings is discipleship. Both the leaders and the group members need to understand this truth so that everyone has the right mindset: we are here to learn to trust and follow Jesus and to make disciples who make disciples. If the purpose is muddy, then the experience will be lacking.

One of the best tools to help both small group leaders and members understand the dynamics of a discipleship-based small group is the material found in the book by Jim Putman and his team called *Real-Life Discipleship Training Manual: Equipping Disciples Who Make Disciples.*[46] I've seen this material transform small groups and churches. Other excellent resources are out there as well. Find some that work well in your context and use them to begin your own discipleship-focused small group.

Remember that getting this close can be incredibly life-changing, but it is also risky. It's a sad truth, but many people in our culture just do not have close relationships. They never talk about their struggles or feelings or what they dream about. They aren't engaged in the mission of Jesus. Even many Christians have spent a great deal of time attending church services but have never experienced Christian relationships. That's what is so wonderful—and challenging—about small groups. As Gigi found, these relationships can be life-changing. As Gigi allowed herself to grow close to fellow Christians, God began to have greater influence in her life.

The personal context is ripe for relational challenges. Many people enter into a small group with misplaced expectations: they want friendships and love, but they do not know how to develop them. This is especially true when relational disappointments and conflicts arise, as they naturally do in a small group. Without guidance, people will pull back in the face of difficulties. They do not understand that they are in a context in which people develop true relationships, and that happens as you work through and resolve conflict. Christlike love is often developed only in the midst of relational struggles.

And at the same time, realize that the Personal Context is not as intimate as some people want. Some people will want deeper relationships than those they experience in a small group. As you'll see in the next chapter, these individuals are looking for the type of relational connection found in the Transparent Context.

Some people will want deeper relationships than those they experience in a small group.

Unfortunately, looking for this kind of relationship can unwittingly become a problem in a small group. That's why it is important to set expectations. While some Transparent Context relationships begin in a small group (a spin-off smaller same-gender group), that kind of depth usually develops outside of the official small group meeting times. Don't make the mistake of expecting transparent and intimate friendships in the Personal Context, especially when you are first getting to know others.

Over time, as relationships deepen, the lines will begin to blur and intimate details will be shared. Smaller transparent groups will naturally form. But that development is not always cut and dried. Typically we'll experience this relational depth in overlapping contexts, where we relate to the same people in both the Transparent and Personal Contexts. In these situations, however, we must be careful to avoid sharing intimate details with those who aren't in a Transparent Context relationship with us. One of the reasons for this lack of full disclosure, like that often experienced in the Transparent Context, is that both men and women tend to feel hesitant about opening up in the presence of the opposite sex. Two or three men or two or three women, alone, over time, often will share about their lives more freely than in the larger group.

Most important, learn to expect (and even welcome) relational conflict.
When people enter into the Personal Context, they can easily trample on
each other and create conflict. People get disappointed with each other.
We all struggle in different ways, and when you put struggling people
together, sparks can fly.

The biggest disappointments come when people have idealistic
expectations of relational harmony and those dreams collide with the
hard realities of sinful human nature. A small group is an ideal place to
practice Christlike love, which means extending grace and forgiveness to
one another rather than imposing unrealistic expectations on others.

Lets talk about Christlike love. As Jesus pointed out, it is *the hallmark*
of true discipleship: "By this all people will know that you are my disciples,
if you have love for one another" (John 13:35). It is fundamentally important to understand that the small group context is where people will
learn to love in the way that Jesus described. And as Jesus and the New
Testament show us, it requires overcoming relational difficulties: it means
forgiveness, patience, kindness, longsuffering, and so on (1 Cor. 13:4–8).
The development of Christlike love is one of the most important foundations and goals of a small group. Help people to embrace the reality of
needing to overcome relational trials. It is worth it.

Spiritual Practices for the Personal Context

The particular things you do in the Personal Context will vary depending
on your local church setting and culture and your particular role in the
group. In what follows, we want to offer some essential practices for cultivating healthy discipleship in the small group context:

- *Prayer.* Pray for everyone in your group specifically by name
  every week. If everyone in the church simply belonged to a small
  group who prayed for everyone in that small group every week, the
  church would see increasing transformation. Just imagine being
  prayed for by a dozen people every week! You can start by writing
  down everyone's prayer requests during your weekly gathering.

- *Consistency.* Another major practice of a small group disciple
  is simply showing up. Just coming every week helps build

relationships. The week-in, week-out humdrum establishes a certain level of trust; then when something interrupts everyday life, whether for good or for bad, you will have an opportunity to help or be helped with words of encouragement and acts of service.

- *Service.* Every Christian should find ways of serving other Christians, because Jesus told us to! "Now that I, your Lord and Teacher, have washed your feet, you also should wash one another's feet" (John 13:14). The small group is a great place to serve one another on a regular basis. If you don't know how to serve those in your small group, just ask people how you can help them! If they don't know, ask God. There is a way you can serve, guaranteed. Otherwise, Jesus' principle of serving as the way to become great applies only to some people.

- *"Unofficial" hangout time.* While the Personal Context is often connected to a structured meeting schedule, small group relationships can and should extend beyond these formal times. If you want to develop close relationships with those in your small group, you should try to make time to hang out with them outside of the group's regular meeting time. That's what Jesus did with his disciples, and there is no reason you shouldn't do it too.

If you are a small group leader, know that you are the one responsible for listening to the Spirit's guidance and helping people trust and follow Jesus. It is a highly relational role, but it also means helping the group navigate some crucial decisions such as setting the time and place and establishing the atmosphere. It also includes a few regular responsibilities that can be adapted based on your unique context:

- *Come prepared to lead the discussion.* Whether you have a word from the Lord for the group, a specific Bible passage to study, or curriculum to discuss, you as the leader are responsible for the direction of the group discussion. Be prepared!

- *Set the vision and give direction.* "Where there is no vision, the people perish," says the proverb (Prov. 29:18 KJV). For your group to move forward in a meaningful way, it needs vision. This vision comes from the Lord through the leader, who takes into account the needs of the people. The vision and direction of the group can be given at every group meeting, and still people will need a refresher the next time. Just when you're getting tired of communicating the vision, people are starting to catch it.

- *Chase the lost sheep.* In nearly every group, you will have people who get ignored, get hurt, or lose interest. Your job as the leader is to be aware of these individuals and respond appropriately. If you see someone slipping away, they might just be done with the group. Perhaps, though, they need to be chased after. Either you or someone else can do the chasing. Use discernment in deciding whether to seek after them yourself or to ask someone who has a good relationship with them to bring them in. To be aware of stragglers and respond appropriately, you need to know the people in your group, and that takes time and shared experiences together.

For most people, as they learn what it means to be a disciple and hear and see what that looks like in the lives of those in the group, it will look radically different from the world around them.

> **Just when you're getting tired of communicating the vision, people are starting to catch it.**

Over time, their lives will change. And the changes needed to follow Jesus today include shifting priorities and adjusting schedules. Christians who are newly embracing the commands of Jesus may find that certain areas of their lives require an overhaul.

The level of commitment to your group will vary based on circumstances, but healthy and close small groups generally meet once a week. This is usually in addition to attending a church service, unless you are meeting as a missional community or house church. To prioritize these relationships, you will need to schedule the times you meet and keep them on the calendar. When sports and hobbies compete, you may need to choose the relationships in your group over other options. Discipleship—growing in relationship with Jesus together—requires as much consistency as playing sports does, perhaps even more!

PUTTING THE PLAN INTO ACTION

Where the rubber meets the road, what we are doing is investing our time in developing significant relationships. This investment usually maxes out at about a dozen people. Why? Because that's all most of us can really handle. Maintaining the relational quality of a small group requires explicit commitment from all involved.

And as we noted earlier, the healthiest small groups spend time together during the everyday activities of life as well as the special events. These include birthdays and graduations and parties, and having your fellow group members there will begin to feel natural as you come to count these individuals as friends. Jesus called his disciples friends (John 15:15), and we should too!

As in the Social Context, sharing meals together is a common, natural way to build relationships with others. If you want to take a step forward in this context, you can take inventory by asking yourself, "How many meals have I shared with that person?"

Here are some other questions you can ask to assess your level of involvement:

- What do I know about their life outside of church?
- What do they struggle with in life?
- What skills and gifts do they have?
- Who are their friends?
- What do they enjoy doing in general?

These simple questions reveal a lot about your relationship with someone. At first, you may be surprised how little you actually know about people in your small group community. Answering these questions will help you measure the level of relationship you have with them. Then you can move forward in cultivating an authentic friendship with them.

All close spiritual community begins with spending time together. This takes sacrifice, but what better model do we have than Jesus Christ, who left the immediate presence of the Father in heaven to live among us! The incarnation

All close spiritual community begins with spending time together.

of Christ, his coming to earth in bodily form, is one of the most scandalous aspects of his ministry as the Son of God. His sacrifice on the cross was possible only because of his sacrifice to take on human form. Entering into the lives of others is emulating Jesus. Helping people trust and follow Jesus means being like Jesus: we initiate relationships, we spend time with people, we teach people, and we invite them to commit their lives to God at deeper and deeper levels.

The Coaching Huddle

Let's add another application for the small group context. In missional communities, coaching huddles are small groups of same-gender leaders who come together for discipleship. In this way, they provide the backbone for the missional community. They ensure that discipleship is the engine driving missional engagement.[47] These huddles consist of six to twelve leaders or emerging leaders who meet regularly for encouragement and accountability. Consequently, both genuine support and robust challenge are offered at different times.

A coaching huddle enables leaders to build character, develop skills, deepen theology, and multiply ministry. While the meetings cover all sorts of ground, in these contexts, Alex and I keep bringing it back to these two questions:

1. What is Jesus saying to you?
2. What are you doing in response?

These two questions emphasize listening to and obeying Jesus in a small group, which is the essence of discipleship. Membership in these groups is by invitation of the leader only—someone can't just bring a friend along with them. Moreover, the coaching huddle needs to meet regularly in order to build continuity and momentum. Each coaching huddle lasts roughly sixty to ninety minutes, although you need to do what works for your context. Clearly, group size and maturity will impact the length of the meeting as well. Group members commit to the huddle with the recognition that it is a place of intentional openness and authenticity leading to significant life change. As the leader, you will set the bar for this commitment.

The expectation is that the coaching huddle will multiply leaders and multiply the impact of communities in God's kingdom. This happens as members of the coaching huddle start their own groups and step out in faith to take new ground (for example, starting a new missional community or taking on new challenges in their workplace). Let us state it one more time: it is about growing disciples who can go and make more disciples.

Let's take a closer look at the key tool used in this group: those two fundamental questions.

The first question, "What is Jesus saying to you?" assumes an important aspect of discipleship, namely that God is speaking to everyone. By asking this simple question, you will get people to think about what God might be saying to them. If God is always talking to his children—and we believe he is—then it's just a matter of discerning what he's actually saying. Asking the question on a regular basis will train leaders and other disciples to be aware of what God is saying to them.

The reason we believe that God is always speaking to us is because of passages like this: "Today, if you hear his voice, do not harden your hearts" (Heb. 3:7–8; 4:7). In our experience, God does indeed speak to us on a regular basis. The point is that whether we hear him clearly or not, we can always be listening. We are given the right to speak to him all the time and every day through prayer, so we can assume that when we are right with him, he will speak back (see Phil. 4:6).

The second question, "What are you doing in response?" is the action step. We can hear from God all we want, but unless we are responding to his call to action, then we're not really disciples. In Matthew 28:20 Jesus told his disciples to teach those in every nation to *know* everything he commanded them.

Well, not exactly. He didn't say that at all. No, he told his disciples to teach those in every nation to *obey* everything he commanded them. Obedience is the mark of a disciple, not knowledge. Again, start with the question, "What is God speaking to you?" and follow that up with the discipleship question, "What are you doing in response?" Even if someone doesn't have a good answer to this question, you're getting them to think about it so that the next time you ask, they will be ready.

Best Practices for Successful Small Group Ministry

Most churches do not focus their small groups on developing leaders for missional communities. For these churches, small groups are the backbone of discipleship in the church. They are the relational and missional focus. We want to take a minute to explore how best to launch these more common small groups in a church setting.

The key to leading a successful group is declaring a clear and compelling purpose from the very beginning. At the end of the first meeting, everyone needs to know the following information:

- The purpose of the group (including direction and goals)
- The boundaries of the group (confidentiality is a must)
- The expectations for the group (behaviors that guide the group)
- The meeting schedule (how often and where the group will meet)
- The role each member is expected to perform (ownership)

You also want to establish roles as the leader. Don't try to do everything yourself, because you will burn yourself out and deprive people of the opportunity to discover and use their spiritual gifts. Here are some of the tasks you can delegate:

- Contacting potential guests
- Arranging for child care
- Coordinating food
- Finding service opportunities
- Hosting meetings
- Sending emails
- Planning extracurricular group events
- Communicating group attendance to the church leadership

Successful groups don't just happen. They are successful because the group experience is cultivated by leaders who carefully and thoughtfully seek the Lord's guidance.

As we conclude this chapter, let's review the following tips for setting up a regular small group meeting. This meeting is to help establish the group's DNA.

- *Pray for God's blessing.* Leading people is an awesome responsibility and a huge challenge. Pray daily for God to give you insight into his Word. Have a servant's heart as you lead your group. If the Lord has called you to lead the group, don't worry about your ability because he will give you the essential skills to lead it.

- *Get personal.* While most of us are now quite email/text/social media savvy, the personal touch of a phone call, either to extend the initial invitation or as a reminder just a day or so prior to the meeting, can have a big impact. Members may feel more comfortable attending if they've had the chance to talk to the leader prior to the first meeting.

- *Understand the context of your first meeting.* People may feel a bit hesitant about being there. Don't be discouraged if they come once but then don't continue. You are testing each other out. Don't expect (or ask for) full-scale openness at first; total candor actually is not healthy in the beginning!

- *Prepare the environment.* Make sure the meeting area is prepared before group members arrive. Leaders should be at the door welcoming guests and assisting; some even use name tags. Review this checklist before the meeting:
    1. Name tags and markers, if appropriate for your setting
    2. No outside noises (cell phones, TVs, etc.)
    3. No pets in the meeting area
    4. Light refreshments or a meal, depending on your context (group members should volunteer to bring refreshments to subsequent meetings)
    5. Seating, lighting, comfortable temperature
    6. Child-care arrangements that are safe and age-appropriate

- *Warm up the group with an icebreaker.* Icebreakers help develop the group's relational component. Early on, they should be light and humorous.

- *Establish a group covenant.* This is an explicit agreement on the purposes of the group, boundaries, expectations, childcare, and so on, as described above. Some leaders draft written copies to review; others just talk it over verbally. The key element is clarity upfront about the group.

- *Allow time for questions.* Clearly state the details of the group. If members sense that you are unclear about the direction of the group, they may back off. Be as specific as you can when answering questions.

- *Pursue your group members after the first meeting.* Often people need personal communication from the leader to realize that they are wanted and valued. A follow-up phone call can provide this reassurance. Your communication with group members is vital to the growth and life of your group.

A healthy Christian community is like a well-watered garden, bringing joy and refreshment to everyone who takes part. Just like a well that provides water, Jesus gives life to all who come to him. As the body of Christ, we are the living hands, feet, and voice of Christ for one another. In this way, close Christian community is essential for your health and the health of those around you. Paul said it well: "The eye cannot say to the hand, 'I don't need you!'" (1 Cor. 12:21). We are all members of the same body, and we need every single part. You are indispensable to those around you!

GETTING STARTED

1. (For church leaders:) If your church is bound to an adult Sunday School model, explore reformatting that model into small groups that meet at that same time. This may be a much easier transition for many churches, especially when their members live busy lives and cannot easily find additional times to meet. Just make sure that it is a relational experience (in addition to Bible study) and that everyone also meets regularly in some fashion outside the Sunday school class. Perhaps the outside meeting will happen every month or two.

2. (For church leaders:) With your leadership team, consider how your small groups, leader huddles, or Sunday school groups can be repositioned to be more explicitly about discipleship.

3. How can you help your existing small group become more focused on discipleship? What would this look like in practice?

4. Teach everyone, repeatedly, to expect relational conflicts and to plan to work through them. How can you help others not to allow relational problems to undermine their group? Is there anyone in your life right now whom you need to forgive? Choose not to allow room for the enemy to operate in that relationship.

5. Do you (or those around you) ever expect to experience a deeper level of closeness in a Personal Context than is realistic? How might a better grasp of the difference in outcomes between the Personal and Transparent Contexts help resolve this issue?

6. How are you deliberately making room for personal support outside of formal meetings? Checking in with your fellow group members now and then is a great way for people to pray for and help each other in the day-to-day affairs of their lives.

ADDITIONAL RESOURCES FOR THE PERSONAL CONTEXT

Coleman, Robert. *Master Plan of Evangelism*. Grand Rapids: Revell, 2010.

Donahue, Bill. *Leading Life-Changing Small Groups*. Grand Rapids: Zondervan, 2012.

Howerton, Rick. *A Different Kind of Tribe: Embracing the New Small-Group Dynamic*. Colorado Springs: NavPress, 2012.

Putman, Jim, and Bobby Harrington. *DiscipleShift: Five Steps That Help Your Church to Make Disciples Who Make Disciples*, Exponential Series. Grand Rapids: Zondervan, 2013.

Putman, Jim, et al. *Real-Life Discipleship Training Manual: Equipping Disciples Who Make Disciples*. Colorado Springs: NavPress, 2010.

Reed, Ben. *Starting Small: The Ultimate Small Group Blueprint*. Rainer Publishing, 2013.

Chapter Ten

WIRED FOR INTIMACY

Understanding the Transparent Context

Key Principle: In the Transparent Context, two to four people form a close bond and discipleship focuses on intimacy, openness, and impact.

TRANSPARENT

I (Bobby) asked a few guys from church to join me for a D-Group (discipleship group) early in the morning before work. Nashville, where we live, is like most major cities in North America: people work fifty-five to sixty hours a week and live crazy-busy lives. They are usually scrambling to make it home in the evening, and when they get there, they have lots of things to do. The three men in the D-Group all had demanding jobs, and two of them had busy families with children. The other man did not have children. The only realistic time we could meet was very early in the morning before work.

I invited the one without children, Jordan, to join us because it was about a year after his baptism and he fit the profile of the kind of person in whom God has called me to invest as a lead pastor—he is available, faithful, teachable, and reliable. He shows all the signs of being a leader with the ability to minister to others. I asked him to pray about joining us, and I knew I had the right man when he said, "I don't need to pray about it; I'm ready to join. When and where do we start?"

Because of my convictions about Jesus and the gospel, I wanted to start, as I always do now, with our Foundations material. As I learned a few years ago, the Jesus we teach and the gospel we uphold determine the disciples we make. I wanted these men to buy in to the real, life-changing Jesus and his wonderful and costly gospel.

We started to get to know each other and before long we were talking about Jesus and our real lives, the transparent lives that men seldom find where they feel safe enough to be authentic. We looked forward to these early-morning meetings. I got to see the best of these three men as we talked about what it really means for them to trust and follow Jesus in the deepest parts of their lives.

The Transparent Context is the closest of the discipling relationships that we experience with other people. There is no hiding here; it is raw, life-on-life interaction. All pretense falls away, and we come to see each other, soul to soul. The discipleship we experience in these relationships is the most powerful because we are so vulnerable and open. Comparing public discipling contexts, people sometimes quip, "You can impress people with ideas and words from a distance, but you can truly impact people only when you are close up." The Transparent Context has the greatest potential for both impact and, paradoxically, disappointment.

There is no hiding here; it is raw, life-on-life interaction.

THE TRANSPARENT CONTEXT

The Transparent Context—typically a group of two to four (and possibly a few more)—normally emerges among those who already have an existing relationship in the Personal, Social, or Public Context. In the Transparent Context, we commit to going deeper, getting beneath the surface. At this level, we don't hide thoughts or feelings or put up barriers. Soon we begin to see each other's hearts. We meet the naked self, which is often hidden in other contexts.

This is where learning to trust and follow Jesus leads to the biggest change in our lives.

The Transparent Context is where we come face-to-face with the flaws and strengths, fears and hopes, disappointments and joys in our own life and the lives of others. It is a wonderful context for discipleship because this is where learning to trust and follow Jesus leads to the biggest change in our lives.

Discipleship at this level typically involves a group of men or a group of women committing to grow in hearing and obeying God together over an extended period of time. In many of the men's groups I've been involved in, it has been described by the words of Proverbs 27:17: "As iron sharpens iron, so one person sharpens another."

Jesus in the Transparent Context

Jesus chose twelve men as his primary disciples, engaging with them in the Personal Context. Then from among the Twelve, he chose three—Peter, James, and John—and gave them an extra measure of his time and attention. He revealed himself to them in ways the others did not see or experience.

We see Peter, James, and John with Jesus in the Transparent Context at key times in the Gospels:

- At the healing of Peter's mother-in-law (Mark 1:29–31)
- At the raising of Jairus's daughter from the dead (Mark 5:37–43)
- On the Mount of Transfiguration, where they saw Moses, Elijah, and then Jesus as God commended Jesus to them and told them to "listen to him" (Mark 9:2–13)
- On the Mount of Olives where Jesus described the destruction of the temple and end-time events (Luke 21:5–38)
- At the garden of Gethsemane, where they were invited to pray with Jesus and see him at his most vulnerable private moment (Matt. 26:37–38)

In particular, the Gospels show us that Jesus seems to have had an especially close and intimate friendship with Peter. Peter, of course, was the one who walked on water in the storm, who swam to shore from the boat, and who confessed Jesus as the Christ. These examples reveal just how much positive growth can happen in Transparent Context relationships. Peter learned that he could trust Jesus during these mountaintop experiences. And Jesus could see the deeper heart struggles of Peter.

As is common in the Transparent Context, the relationship between Jesus and Peter was also filled with tension. As Jesus was arrested and his death approached, Peter had doubts and misunderstandings about

Jesus. Whatever the cause, we know that Peter was afraid to associate himself with Jesus too closely. The same night that he said, "I will lay down my life for you," he also said, "I don't know the man!" (John 13:37; Matt. 26:72). Not only did Jesus, as the disciple maker, receive great love and faith from Peter, but he also was greatly hurt by Peter's denials.

At this level, we see the real person—warts and all—because our sin, selfishness, and shallowness cannot be hidden.

Such is the nature of intimate discipling relationships. Ups and downs are to be expected. The life shared in this context is not always appropriate to reveal in more public contexts. At this level, we see the real person—warts and all—because our sin, selfishness, and shallowness cannot be hidden.

Other Biblical Examples

The Bible contains many examples of transparent relationships:

- Moses with Joshua and Aaron, learning together (Exod. 17:9–10, 12)
- Eli with Samuel as Samuel raised up and trained the young man (1 Sam. 3:1–18)
- Samuel with David, guiding him up close and personal (1 Sam. 16:13; 19:18)
- Elijah with Elisha, mentoring him to take Elijah's role (1 Kings 19:19)
- Paul with Titus and Silas (in addition to Timothy) in the great work of planting and developing churches (2 Cor. 8:23; 12:18; Gal. 2:3; Acts 15:40; 16:25)
- Barnabas with John Mark in their ministries together (Acts 15:39)

The apostle Paul seems to teach the role of transparent discipling relationships in 2 Timothy 2:2: "And the things you have heard me say in the presence of many witnesses entrust to reliable people who will also be qualified to teach others." In this passage, we see four generations of disciples:

1. Paul was discipled by visions from Jesus and teaching from the other apostles.

2. Paul discipled Timothy.

3. Timothy is called to disciple reliable people.

4. The reliable people discipled by Timothy are to disciple others.

We believe these relations point to Transparent Context discipleship because Paul's letters indicate that he had an intimate relationship with Timothy, and in his exhortation he encourages Timothy to pass along the things he has learned from Paul to others in this same context of close, intimate relationship.

Paul goes on to describe the up close and personal nature of this kind of discipling relationship in 2 Timothy 3:10–12: "You, however, know all about my teaching, my way of life, my purpose, faith, patience, love, endurance, persecutions, sufferings—what kinds of things happened to me in Antioch, Iconium and Lystra, the persecutions I endured. Yet the Lord rescued me from all of them. In fact, everyone who wants to live a godly life in Christ Jesus will be persecuted."

Paul mentions several of the key elements of the Transparent Context here. He speaks of his teaching, his way of life, and his life's purpose, including examples of how he exercised faith, patience, and endurance—especially in the face of persecution and suffering. These were things Paul spoke about publicly, to be sure, but we know that Timothy knew Paul intimately, similar to the way in which Peter, James, and John knew Jesus. This is life impartation, or as some call it, life-on-life discipleship. It's what Paul was referring to when he told the Corinthians, "Therefore I urge you to imitate me" (1 Cor. 4:16). In this relational context, Paul was imparting his life to Timothy, not just information about Jesus.

The Transparent Context is the relational setting in which I (Bobby) have had the most fruitfulness in developing leaders in the local church. Close-up, life-on-life relationships like these are where God forges Christlike character and deep spiritual understanding.

When I planted Harpeth Christian Church, the Transparent Context is where the enduring leaders were developed. JP, our first staff member, is a good example. Once we were established as a church, JP proudly joined the staff to take care of office administration and our portable church setup each week (we met in a school). Over time, JP and I got to know each other at a deep level. We met for planning, follow-up, and sermon development. We laughed, cried, disagreed, and worked it out. In all of it, I constantly sought to show him the teachings of the Bible.

Like Timothy with Paul, JP saw my teaching, my way of life, and my purpose. He eventually took over the youth ministry at our church. After serving for over a decade as a youth minister with us, he moved to Uganda, where he is now helping to lead a network of hundreds of churches. He never went to seminary or received a Bible degree, but he learned ministry in the same way that Timothy learned it from Paul.

To this day, the most effective leadership development we are witnessing in our church is the discipleship based on the principles of transparent discipling relationships. This is the way our most effective elders, small group leaders, and staff have been developed. We believe local church pastors are called to raise up and equip leaders, and they must do so in the Transparent Context. Yes, Bible colleges and seminaries can help in many ways, but leadership development in life-on-life relationships, in which more mature leaders disciple less mature leaders, is God's plan for deep transformation.

We see an example of a life-on-life relationship in the Old Testament in the intimate friendship between David and Jonathan. From an early age, these two men were close friends. The Bible doesn't give us the specific details as to why they became friends, but we do know that they were so close that "the soul of Jonathan was knit to the soul of David" (1 Sam. 18:1 ESV). Friendship doesn't get any closer than that!

This friendship became important for David as he was called by God to the kingship of Israel. Saul, the current king and Jonathan's father, was jealous of David, which caused major tension in the relationships between the three men. On three different occasions, Saul tried to kill David with a spear! Saul's outrageous behavior put his son Jonathan in an awkward position, because Jonathan was torn between loyalty to his father and loyalty to his best friend. The conflict between Saul and David came to a head, and Jonathan helped David to escape from death. When David left, he and Jonathan wept together, "David weeping the most" (1 Sam. 20:41 ESV).

Then Jonathan told David, "Go in peace, because we have sworn both of us in the name of the LORD, saying, 'The LORD shall be between me and you, and between my offspring and your offspring, forever'" (20:42 ESV).

The bond between these two men was formed around God himself, and this relationship helped David to move through one of the most difficult seasons of his life, during which King Saul was continually trying to kill him. What better time than that to have a good friend! Their friendship is a vivid illustration of the proverb, "There is a friend who sticks closer than a brother" (Prov. 18:24).

Not only are friendships like David and Jonathan's beautiful expressions of brotherly love characterized by mutual encouragement, but they are also the place where confrontation can be used powerfully by God to form Christ in our lives. God uses our relational conflicts with others to reveal our blind spots, to teach us grace and forgiveness, and to show us what it means to be faithful in walking with one another through the good, the bad, and the ugly of life.

> God uses our relational conflicts with others to reveal our blind spots, to teach us grace and forgiveness, and to show us what it means to be faithful in walking with one another through the good, the bad, and the ugly of life.

Because of the close connection we experience with others at this level, God uses this place of trust and vulnerability to break through some of the deepest struggles and sins within us.

Returning to the life of David, we see the principle of beneficial confrontation at work within another friendship of David's. The prophet Nathan was a good friend and trusted advisor to David. Though both men loved the Lord, their friendship didn't mean they always agreed with one another. At one point Nathan was called by God to confront David about his sin and hypocrisy (2 Sam. 12:1–10).

DISCIPLESHIP IN THE TRANSPARENT CONTEXT

Many effective models of transparent discipleship are being used today. One thing to note in what follows is that almost all the discipleship practitioners using this context in a local church advocate same-gender groups.[48] Let's take a look at four noteworthy practitioners and the different ways they lead people into a closer walk with Jesus. There are dozens of popular examples in addition to the following models.

1. Neil Cole (Life Transformation Groups)

Neil Cole found great success in starting what he calls "Life Transformation Groups" or LTGs, and many others have adopted this model for discipleship. Neil describes his formula in the book *Search and Rescue*.[49] LTGs are groups of two to four people of the same gender who get together on a weekly basis. They meet for an hour to ninety minutes to do three simple things:

1. Answer specific accountability questions from each other.

2. Pray for the lost specifically by name.

3. Discuss the thirty chapters of the Bible they all read that week.

The beauty of LTGs is twofold. First, they are simple and reproducible. Their three focal points are core practices for Christians and clearly define the structure of each meeting. Second, LTGs involve a high level of accountability. Not only are members held accountable for sin and encouraged to pray for the lost, but when one person doesn't read the assigned thirty chapters, everyone is affected because all are required to reread the chapters until everyone has read them all during the same week.

2. Robby Gallaty (D-Groups)

Robby leads Long Hollow Baptist Church in Hendersonville, Tennessee, but has found a way to make church life very organic and discipleship based. Robby is helping this megachurch replicate the experience of the last church he led in Chattanooga, where a high percentage of the people in the church were engaged in weekly D-Groups. Robby describes his formula in the book *Growing Up*.[50] Like LTGs, D-Groups are made up of two to four people of the same gender who get together weekly. They meet for an hour or more to do four basic things:

1. HEAR from God's Word (Bible reading; HEAR stands for Highlight, Explain, Apply, Respond)
2. Hide (Scripture memorization)
3. Honor (prayer)
4. Help (obedience)

3. Randy Pope (Life-on-Life Groups)

Randy built the influential Perimeter Church in Atlanta around Life-on-Life groups. They have used this system for many years and currently disciple over four thousand people weekly; they've also planted more than forty churches. Life-on-life groups have proven to be a very effective discipleship format. The group size can be four people, but they can also be as big as twelve people. Like the other groups in the transparent context, they are same-gender groups. Pope refers to their structure with the acronym TEAMS.[51]

- *Truth:* learning what God has revealed for his people to know, understand, and obey.
- *Equipping:* massaging God's truth into life so that it becomes understandable and usable.
- *Accountability:* asking the hard questions to encourage living fully for Christ.
- *Mission:* engaging with the lost world in order to impart the gospel through word and deed.
- *Supplication:* engaging in conversation with God to express dependence on him.

4. Tara-Leigh Cobble (Women's D-Groups)

Tara-Leigh was discipled by Matt and Lauren Chandler, and she went on to found an organization called D-Group, short for "discipleship group."[52] These small groups are for women around the country who are committed to a local church but want to go deeper in their relationship with the Lord. These women get together for two hours each week and go through a common curriculum. They read and memorize Scripture, read a workbook, and listen to podcasts. Many of the groups are bigger than the Transparent size (more than five women), but the processes are applicable in the Transparent Context.[53]

GOALS FOR DISCIPLESHIP IN THE TRANSPARENT CONTEXT

As with the other contexts, we want to highlight the three outcomes associated with the Transparent Context. The three key goals and expectations you should have for discipleship in this context are *intimacy*, *openness*, and *impact*.

Goal 1: Intimacy

We realize that the word *intimacy* is fine for some but for others sounds a bit too touchy-feely. When used around men, they may roll their eyes and tune out. But that's our hang-up. The word is used by sociologists to describe the closest of human relationships in a way that means "up close and personal" or "heart to heart." It describes something that takes time to develop, but when that quality is developed, it is incredibly powerful. Let me explain what I mean by that.

As we mentioned earlier, in our Western context, our primary discipleship methods have been educational in focus. The goal is on acquiring information. In this approach people read the Bible, memorize Scripture verses, and sometimes even take tests. While these can be good practices, we should not equate them with biblical discipleship. A strictly educational approach doesn't describe the discipleship method of either Jesus or Paul (or any of the apostles).

But there is a quick and easy way to describe what they did. It's the word *intimacy*.

Intimacy means that we live with vulnerability. And while sharing in this way is difficult, growing and maturing while doing so is even harder. A helpful image I

Intimacy means that we live with vulnerability.

use to communicate the concept of vulnerability is a fishbowl. The metaphor breaks down in places, but it's one we are all familiar with. In a fishbowl, our lives are visible to everyone. There is no place to hide. And when it comes to discipleship, we need to see that the *only* way we can grow is by being open and vulnerable.

This kind of intimacy is inappropriate in larger contexts. In public, for example, most people don't naturally share their worst sins or most embarrassing moments. We don't spill our guts out to the entire church. On the contrary, God calls us to this level with just a few people in a context of mutual love, respect, and trust.

We all know what happens when our intimate secrets and failures are exposed. We've seen the fallout from these situations with presidents and preachers alike. And while we hope that the church will always be a loving, grace-filled community, the truth is that we might struggle to feel that love and grace in a Public Context gathering. Even in the Social and Personal Contexts there are challenges. But in the supportive and confidential environment of a Transparent Context discipling relationship, vulnerability is not shameful and destructive but rather helpful and life-giving.

Think of Jesus intimately sharing his life in this context. We need to keep in mind that he never sinned, but the Bible is clear that he experienced pain and disappointment and that he let his close disciples see these struggles. Jesus allowed Peter, James, and John to be in his life, up close and personal, day after day. They were able to listen to his teaching as they walked along the road with the other disciples. They watched him go off to pray early in the morning (Mark 1:35). And they were with him, alone or with one or two others, to see the man the crowds never saw. They saw him in the garden of Gethsemane, praying to his Father, and heard the cries and concerns of his heart.

Up to this point, we've spoken of discipleship primarily in the context of broader relationships, such as our neighborhoods or networks of friends outside of our family. But discipleship occurs in the home, with our family, as well. The parent-child relationship is the first and most natural discipling relationship. In Deuteronomy 6 we read about this kind of life-on-life discipleship: "These words that I command you today shall be on your heart. You shall teach them diligently to your children, and shall talk of them when you sit in your house, and when you walk by the way, and when you lie down, and when you rise" (6:6–7 ESV).

The Bible says that parents should disciple their children, and that is exactly what Jesus did with his close disciples.[54] He talked about God while they were sitting in the house, walking on the road, lying down, and getting up. His whole life was open to his disciples for learning. The vignette of Jesus' vulnerability in the garden of Gethsemane shows us potentially the most crucial decision point in Jesus' life. As God's Son, he allowed his desires to be known in the garden. It is likely that, while the disciples eventually fell asleep, they still heard Jesus' prayer, and that's the original source of his prayer, "Take this cup from me; yet not my will, but yours be done" (Luke 22:42).

Earlier we mentioned that disappointment is common in the Transparent Context (more on that in the next chapter). And here we can see Jesus expressing his own disappointment. In his most challenging moment, Jesus has placed his authority and confidence on the line with his three closest disciples. And they have not guarded him; they have not stood with him through the trials of the night. They will soon run away from him.

Considering that Jesus is the ultimate disciple maker, we can find some solace in the fact that his best friends left him at the most crucial moment of his life. The soldiers came and the disciples scattered like sheep without a shepherd. Though Jesus knew this would happen, he was vulnerable anyway. He didn't escape or hide away. He pressed in, and that gave his disciples courage to do the same later in their lives.

Goal 2: Openness

Jesus' disciples felt free to be themselves around him. They were comfortable asking bold questions about their standing with him. James and John offer an interesting example of this boldness. They understood that Jesus was setting up a kingdom, and they wanted good positions when the kingdom was finally established. So they came to Jesus with their mother and told him, "Teacher, we want you to do for us whatever we ask" (Mark 10:35). Jesus asked in reply, "What do you want me to do for you?" These two proceeded to ask for the two best positions of power in the kingdom, to sit on his right and his left. Jesus challenged their understanding of what this meant and told them it wasn't for him to decide those positions. A dispute broke out among the other ten disciples, and Jesus used the chaos to teach them about authority and servanthood.

Our point in sharing this example is not to encourage self-seeking grabs for power. It's to show that the disciples felt comfortable enough to express their true desires, even if they were under-informed! If trust is a two-sided coin, the two sides of the coin are openness and authenticity. With one but not the other, you cannot have a trusting relationship. You can be open with someone, but if you are not authentic in your interactions with them, trust will not characterize your relationship. While these two elements of trust building are *present* at all levels of relationship—public, social, personal—they are *vital* in the intimate context of relationship. One betrayal has the potential to destroy an intimate relationship. Just think about honesty in the marriage relationship (another Transparent Context relationship). While trust eventually can be reestablished, a breach of trust damages the desire to be known and to share intimate connection until trust is rebuilt.

While full public disclosure can feel bad, secrecy is not healthy either. As disciples of Jesus, we are called to confess our sins to each other and live in true vulnerability—not with everyone but with the few (James 5:16). This is true in discipling relationships as well. As you learn to hear from God in this context, often he will ask you to be more than just vulnerable with people, but to be completely open with a select few (more on how to do that in the next chapter).

But honesty includes more than just confessing sin or revealing weakness! You can be honest about your victories and strengths too. The powerful impact of intimate relationship is clear in the sharing of good moments. Take a look at Jesus' relationship with Peter, for example. Although Peter denied Jesus three times, Jesus still made him a pillar of the early church. What may have been the most shameful night of Peter's life turned into the brightest day for Peter's future. Peter had denied Jesus three times around a late-night charcoal fire. Jesus reinstated Peter three times on the beach of Galilee near Capernaum after his resurrection. He redeemed the broken relationship in a personally meaningful way to Peter. In contrast with that frightful and desperate night, Jesus chose the opposite setting to affirm Peter: a charcoal fire in the morning light. These two scenes, of denial and affirmation, contain the only two occurrences of "charcoal fire" in the New Testament! Nowhere else is this type of fire mentioned. It was no coincidence that Jesus cooked breakfast over the same kind of fire Peter stood near during the denials. The impact on Peter was powerful. You can feel the strong emotions by reading these two lines:

1. "As soon as Simon Peter heard [John] say, 'It is the Lord,' . . . [he] jumped into the water" and swam to shore (John 21:7).

2. "Peter was hurt because Jesus asked him the third time, 'Do you love me?'" (John 21:17).

Peter's redemption was vital for him and for the church, and it happened out of an intimate connection with Jesus.

Goal 3: Impact

Encountering Jesus, the living Word of God, transformed Peter's life. And one of the best ways we can disciple others is by digging into the written Word of God with the help of the Holy Spirit, whereby God can speak to us personally. Discipleship is helping people trust and follow Jesus as Lord, and it requires that we both *understand* the truth and *obey* it. What we know matters only if it translates into how we live.

Discipleship relationships in the Transparent Context are about helping people change through the power of the Word and the Spirit in the choices we make and the actions we take. Acknowledging Jesus' lordship involves internalizing the teachings of the Bible so they inform and shape our desires. This requires a degree of discernment as well as a warfare mentality. The apostle Paul described it this way in 2 Corinthians 10:5: "We demolish arguments and every pretension that sets itself up against the knowledge of God, and we take captive every thought to make it obedient to Christ."

Notice that last phrase, "We take captive every thought to make it obedient to Christ." Paul helped people to trust and follow Jesus by teaching them to take every thought captive and then make it obedient to Christ. If obedience to Jesus Christ is our goal, we must disciple people in God's way of thinking. In Romans 12:2–3 the apostle Paul instructed, "Do not conform to the pattern of this world, but be transformed by the renewing of your mind. Then you will be able to test and approve what God's will is—his good, pleasing and perfect will."

Transformation, according to Paul, is grounded in the renewing of the mind. A renewed mind leads to a changed life and the ability to know—at a heart level—what pleases God. Knowledge is not the end or the primary focus of discipleship, but it still is vitally important. How we think is the biggest determiner of how we live, because what we believe shapes what we want and what we do. Knowledge leads to changes in the way we act; as we consistently follow the Lord, we learn what pleases him, seeing it as good, pleasing, and perfect. A major part of discipleship is getting people into the Bible and helping them to study it in a way that leads to action.[55]

> **Knowledge is not the end or the primary focus of discipleship, but it still is vitally important.**

If we are not applying biblical truth to a person's real everyday life, it is not true discipleship. Second Timothy 3:16–17 describes the role Scripture should play in the life of a disciple: "All Scripture is God-breathed and is useful for teaching, rebuking, correcting and training in righteousness, so that the servant of God may be thoroughly equipped for every good work."

The goal of Scripture is to equip God's people "for every good work." Again, the true test of helping people to know the Bible is how they apply and live out the Bible's teachings.

Discipleship is practical. In the Transparent Context, we help each other in the nitty-gritty world of our real beliefs, attitudes, and habits. We help each other both to understand and to follow the teachings of Scripture. It is at this level, for example, that a man learns that pornography is wrong and gets help in overcoming his addiction to it. It is at this level that a woman learns how to love her husband and honor him, even when she feels that he isn't meeting her needs. And it is at this level that people learn how to cast their daily cares and anxieties onto Jesus and how to pray effectively.

THE TRANSPARENT CONTEXT: WHERE MOST TRANSFORMATION OCCURS

Of all the contexts of discipleship, the Transparent Context is where the most transformation takes place. Yet that doesn't diminish the value of the other contexts; on the contrary, each supports and nurtures the others. Taking away any one of the contexts results in a lopsided community. We need the deep *and* the wide contexts for growth in Christ, just as we can learn how "wide and long and high and deep is the love of Christ" (Eph. 3:18). Deep personal transformation happens in close relationships with just a few, because only a few people can earn the trust it takes to be vulnerable, open, and honest in life-on-life situations.

Chapter Eleven

BUILDING THE CLOSEST RELATIONSHIPS

Discipleship in the Transparent Context

Key Application: Start discipleship groups that bring clusters of men or clusters of women together to help and encourage people to form deep connections.

When I (Bobby) first planted Harpeth Christian Church, I was so happy when we could hire staff. In my mind, once I was able to hire staff, their role would be to take on different parts of the ministry and free me up to do more of what I enjoyed the most and did the best.

Because we were a young church and not able to offer big salaries, we often hired young leaders. We thought their youth and enthusiasm would make up for their lack of maturity and experience. We hired them, made their job descriptions clear, and then set them loose.

The problem with this plan is that I did not disciple them. And no one else was there to disciple them. They often failed, and it was my fault.

Eventually I realized that as the lead pastor I was responsible for personally discipling those on my staff until we became a church that was large enough that others could help take over this vital role with some of the staff. They would practice only what I taught and modeled for them. These men formed my most important D-Group.

We created four regular contexts for transparent discipleship every week. These contexts are in addition to the one-on-one meetings I have with them (the meetings where I specifically model practices for them to replicate).

175

- We met for breakfast every Tuesday morning from 7:00 to 8:30 with our Bibles to have an unplanned talk and bring up whatever is on our minds. The staff members who are in their twenties especially love this time.

- We pray together at a heart-to-heart level for one hour every Wednesday, starting at 11:00 a.m.

- They join our Leadership and Ordination class every Friday from 6:30 to 8:00 a.m. with about fifteen other men. This time together includes in-depth Bible study, Scripture memorization, and required readings.

- We get together fairly regularly for pizza, poker (betting just on chips), or social gatherings, which include days when we just have fun.

These four gatherings were in addition to regular Sundays at church, taking them on special trips to learn more about discipleship, and so on. This close level of relationship is a reflection of our efforts to replicate in our leadership culture the types of transparent discipleship that Jesus demonstrated. The Transparent Context is the most important leadership development context in our church.

To create intentional strategies and practices in the Transparent Context, you will need to consider several key principles. Do not think of the staff discipleship I have just been describing, but the people in your community or church whom you want to disciple as a pastor or everyday church leader. First is the question of *who*. How do you decide who will be in your group?

We design our discipleship groups (D-Groups) to help people come to faith or grow up in their faith—or both. We select disciples by asking four vital questions:

1. *With whom could I form a discipling relationship?* These could be people in your neighborhood, people at work, or people in the church. We are looking for relationships that seem to have good interaction, even good chemistry.

2. *Who is receptive to me?* Who easily listens to me and shows interest in what I have to say about the things of Jesus? Again, this could be a non-Christian or a Christian. Our friend Dave Buehring puts it this way when he talks to us about discipleship: "In whose ears are your words big?"[56]

3. *Who is a good investment?* This is a hard question, especially if the person is not yet a Christian. But in the church, it is the wise question. Is the person I'm thinking about discipling available, faithful, teachable, and reliable (or AFTR, as in *AFTeR Jesus*, but shortened)? This kind of person makes my investment of time and friendship a good and wise one. If you are a church leader, these are especially important considerations.

4. *Is God in it?* Do I feel God nudging me toward anyone in particular? Do I naturally have the sense that God might be leading me to someone? Is it a leading that might serve as the foundation of a discipling relationship?

As you can see, these questions can be fairly subjective, but we seek to make them Spirit led. They depend on some level of affinity for the person, perhaps some shared experiences, or at the very least a desire to spend time together and grow together. Often these are people we've met or gotten to know in one of the other relational contexts, though we may not know them beyond the Social or Public Context.

If someone meets all the criteria indicated by these questions, then we find we are more likely to have a significant impact in discipling them in the Transparent Context.

GUIDELINES FOR DISCIPLESHIP IN THE TRANSPARENT CONTEXT

We'd like to offer three guidelines that can help you to have a successful discipleship ministry in the Transparent Context. These guidelines flow out of the outcomes we highlighted in the previous chapter. As the leader, you will want to model these guidelines.

1. Reveal Your Intimate Thoughts

Remember, *intimate* means up close and very personal. Reaching this level of closeness takes time. But discipleship as practiced by Jesus, Paul, and the other leaders in the New Testament often occurred in this context. Groups need to be set up from the beginning with this underlying philosophy in mind.

My co-minister, Josh Patrick, starts his groups with a specific life-on-life, heart-to-heart, intimacy-encouraging process. Josh has every person in his group take turns telling his spiritual life story. He gives them a short assignment to complete before the meeting that includes the following:

> Look through the rearview mirror at your life. What would be some *defining moments* where you can see the fingerprints of God? What moments had a profound impact on the direction of your life?
>
> Now take those defining moments and narrow them down to five or so. Take each of these moments and write a paragraph or two elaborating on it. You have now written your story, telling how God has worked in your life to shape you into who you are today for the sake of his purpose in you.

Each man comes into the meeting with his notes, which are based on the outline Josh has given them beforehand. This strategy works because developing intimacy is not a mechanical process. Telling stories not only reveals facts and details of a person's life but also shows us how they see themselves, what they value, how they think, and what motivates them. Getting to know a person is largely a matter of learning their story. That's why the sharing of stories in a D-Group like this one helps people to connect relatively quickly.

Josh leads people with vulnerability and models the expectations of this context out of his own openness. He encourages those in his D-Group to look back at their lives and share where they've come from, and then he coaches them through an exercise to help them determine where they want to go in life.

Finally he gives them one more starting exercise: creating a spiritual obituary describing how they want their lives to end. Josh sets the example by first sharing his own obituary, as he imagines it might be one day, with those in his newly formed D-Group. He has given us permission to share one part of it with you. It is Josh's description of what his wife, Joni, will say about him after he has finished his time on earth. He imagines Joni saying:

> When I met Josh, he was a seriously flawed and deeply broken man, but as the years went by, I personally witnessed God raise him from the dead. Josh was fully alive because he was fully surrendered to Jesus. He may have accomplished a lot as a communicator and disciple maker, but he never wavered from his core passion—*to know Jesus*—intimately and personally. He was obsessed with knowing and being known by Jesus and helping others experience these same things. His main purpose in life was to trust and follow Jesus wherever he happened to be at the moment. He loved me extravagantly and sacrificially. He loved our daughters and taught and modeled the way of Jesus to them. We are all blessed and profoundly grateful to have shared life with Josh.

At this level of vulnerable sharing, we are able to help each other trust and follow Jesus at the deepest levels of our lives. We are being real with one another about the most important things in life. Establishing a D-Group on a foundation of openness and intimacy enables group members to share the challenges and joys of life at a more profound level.

Since relationships are the vehicle through which discipleship takes place, members of a D-Group also need to have fun and do things socially together.

Every relationship that matters includes times when we're serious, times when we learn and grow, and times when we have fun and play.

Every relationship that matters includes times when we're serious, times when we learn and grow, and times when we have fun and play. In the Transparent Context we need these times as well, times that aren't structured but are simply focused on relationship building. Sharing a meal, taking a walk or bike ride, going to the movies, playing or watching sports, and many other activities are great ways to strengthen bonds in the Transparent Context.

Over the years I (Bobby) have had the honor of becoming friends with Robert Coleman, who wrote the book *The Master Plan of Evangelism*. We've worked together on several discipleship forums, and he has visited and spoken at my home church. During one particular interaction between him and a younger staff member at our church, I realized that I enjoyed just watching him build a relationship with someone. At the time, Coleman was eighty-six and the young man on staff was in his early twenties. He asked Coleman, "Could you give me some practical advice in how to disciple people?"

Coleman smiled. "Oh, it's simple," he said. "Just find someone who naturally gravitates to you, then spend time with them. Maybe do something fun, like *taking them to a play*."

At this point, I had to laugh. Apparently when Coleman was in his twenties, going to plays was quite the thing to do. And that's what he did at that age, when he first learned how to disciple others. It was a special moment for all of us, because Coleman was being honest, just sharing something that he had done when he was that age.

I mention that interaction because it cemented for me a key understanding about discipleship in the Transparent Context: it is not complicated. Grabbing a meal, watching football, or just meeting someone at their place of work or school will go a long way in establishing a relationship. You might even go to a play. (Yes, that is something that some people still like to do.)

We want to emphasize this point because in our culture, where people tend to be overly busy, skipping this step is all too easy. Planning time just for relationship building and fun is crucial in discipleship.

2. Make It Open

We've already noted that creating a safe and open environment is key to helping people trust and follow Jesus. It works best when the leader purposely and vulnerably sets the example, creates clear expectations up front, and lets people know their role in the discipling process. The best way to lead the group into an atmosphere of openness is to establish ground rules early on. In many groups we start with the question, "What are your expectations for this group?"

Often people will mention things like "acceptance," "a nonjudgmental attitude," and "authenticity." This is a great opportunity to see who says what and then keep those responses in mind as you move forward. In asserting their hopes and dreams, people feel heard and understood.

Then the leader needs to express his or her expectations for the group. If you list very specific expectations, you will want to ask people at the end of that first session whether those expectations are realistic for them.

The best way to lead the group into an atmosphere of openness is to establish ground rules early on.

Being clear up front may save you (and them) difficulty later on, if commitment to the group ethos doesn't live up to your vision. Listening to the group's expectations and then communicating your own expectations and boundaries and asking for buy-in are vital first steps for moving forward in a healthy way.

The "Group Covenant" (fig. 7) is something we've used to help establish openness and protect what is shared with confidentiality.

Keep in mind that transparency breeds transparency and confession breeds confession. As the leader, you not only set the expectations up front but also maintain the focus throughout the entirety of the group. This takes discipline and clear vision on your part. You want to set the example by being open in the early phase of the group and keep up the example by continuing to be vulnerable about your own life.

When you start a group, be sure to cover the following items either in a covenant (as seen earlier) or in a general discussion about expectations. Discuss the need for the following:

- *Complete confidentiality.* What happens in the group stays in the group. Everyone should agree not to gossip or share the group discussions with those outside the group.
- *Regular attendance.* Showing up every week is huge. Unless the members are committed to attending each week, the group will lose momentum and cohesion.
- *Homework.* Oftentimes discipleship groups use a curriculum or material that members will need to work on between meeting

times. If everyone agrees to do the work, it will pay off when you get together for discipleship meetings.

- *Complete transparency.* D-Groups are not the place to hide who you are or what you do. Everything is on the table. If someone isn't ready to confess their struggles with sin, they are not ready for Transparent Context discipleship.

GROUP COVENANT

Where two or three gather together as my followers, I am there among them. (Matthew 18:20)

The purpose of this group is to experience deep, accelerated transformation at the heart level in the context of safe, Christ-centered friendships.

I commit to the following:

1. **REGULAR ATTENDANCE.** I will attend every meeting unless providentially hindered – no exceptions. I understand that I will have to say "no" to important things in order to meet this commitment, and I am willing to do so.

2. **DOING THE WORK.** I will complete the work assigned to the group and will discipline myself to be prepared for our meetings.

3. **COMPLETE TRANSPARENCY.** I recognize that in order to grow in spiritual maturity, I must openly share my life with this group – the good, the bad, and the ugly.

4. **FINISHING WELL.** I understand that the members of this group will make a significant investment in me. Since it is unfair to them for me to quit, I will be fully engaged in the group for the entire season.

5. **TOTAL CONFIDENTIALITY.** I will treat what is shared in our meetings as sacred by keeping our conversations to myself.

6. **LEADING OTHERS.** At some point, I will partner with Jesus in starting a group like this with other men.

7. **PRAYING FOR MY BROTHERS.** I will regularly pray for the guys in this group – specifically for God to give them wisdom, endurance, and an increasing hunger for Him.

Name _____   Date _____

_____   _____

>> FIGURE 7

- *Prayer for one another.* Lifting each other up in prayer every week helps you to have your finger on where God has each person. God may reveal a word to you about someone in the group, and because of the intimate setting and high level of trust, you may be the only one who speaks into them. Agree to pray for one another every week.

If someone isn't ready to confess their struggles with sin, they are not ready for Transparent Context discipleship.

Charles Spurgeon, the great preacher, once described the necessity of prayer for disciples: "God will bless Elijah and send rain on Israel, but Elijah must pray for it. If the chosen nation is to prosper, Samuel must plead for it. If the Jews are to be delivered, Daniel must intercede. God will bless Paul, and the nations shall be converted through him, but Paul must pray. Pray he did without ceasing; his epistles show that he expected nothing except by asking for it. If you may have everything by asking, and nothing without asking, I beg you to see how absolutely vital prayer is, and I beseech you to abound in it."[57]

3. Look for Impact

Bible study and accountability are major components of every D-Group. This is where we explore the truths of the Bible with the desire that they will impact our lives. God is always speaking, and we can always listen to him. Simply by opening God's Word, we can read what God spoke to his people and consider how we can apply his truth to our lives today. We know that all of Scripture is "useful for teaching, rebuking, correcting and training in righteousness" (2 Tim. 3:16). We also know that we sometimes need help from others to obey God. The combination of the Word of God and the people of God leads to significant impact in our lives.

Personal Bible study is essential to ongoing growth wherever you or the person you're discipling is on the journey of faith. Some sections of the Bible particularly encourage us to live with the Scriptures. In Romans 10:14–17 the apostle Paul points out that until we hear and understand the teachings about Jesus Christ, it is impossible to believe in him. The famous nineteenth-century Christian leader D. L. Moody described his spiritual growth this way: "I prayed for faith and thought that someday faith would come down and strike me like lightning. But faith did not seem to come. One day I read in the tenth chapter of Romans, 'Faith cometh by hearing, and hearing by the Word of God.' I had up to this time closed my Bible and prayed for faith. I now opened my Bible and began to study, and faith has been growing ever since."[58]

The key to developing your faith and seeing it grow is continual exposure to the teachings of the Bible, especially those about Jesus Christ.

> **The key to developing your faith and seeing it grow is continual exposure to the teachings of the Bible, especially those about Jesus Christ.**

Hebrews 4:12 teaches this principle: "For the Word of God is alive and active. Sharper than any double-edged sword, it penetrates even to dividing soul and spirit, joints and marrow; it judges the thoughts and attitudes of the heart." And in Isaiah 55:11 God says when his Word goes out to people, "it will not return to me empty, but will accomplish what I desire and achieve the purpose for which I sent it."

If we want the individuals we're discipling to grow and to make more disciples, we have to help them get into the Bible so that the Bible will change them. We must not underestimate the sanctifying and transforming work of God's Word in our lives. The Bible both understood and applied is crucial to effective discipleship. Grace filled accountability is the companion of heartfelt Bible study.

Disciples hear Jesus speak and obey him. Obedience expresses faith and is a fundamental principle of the Christian life. Consider the following Scripture passages:

> Without faith it is impossible to please God, because anyone who comes to him must believe that he exists and that he rewards those who earnestly seek him.
> —*Hebrews 11:6*

> "You will seek me and find me when you seek me with all your heart. I will be found by you," declares the LORD.
> —*Jeremiah 29:13–14*

The best way to come to know God and the teachings of the Bible is to study Scripture with people who will help you apply it.[59] We love the example of the people of Berea described in the book of Acts. In contrast to the Thessalonians, the Bereans searched the Scriptures to see what was true so that they could know the way of God and properly follow him for themselves. In the Bible they are highly commended: "Now the Berean Jews were of more noble character than those in Thessalonica, for they received the message with great eagerness and examined the Scriptures every day to see if what Paul said was true" (Acts 17:11).

Like the Bereans, if we truly want to be noble in God's sight, we must seek to know the truth of Scripture and then obey it. The truths of the Bible that are learned, obeyed, and lived out in the Transparent Context have a tremendous impact on others.

DISCIPLING NON-CHRISTIANS

While it may come as a surprise, we have found that the Transparent Context is one of the best environments in which to help non-Christians process the claims of Jesus and commit their lives to him. If you have a good relationship with someone and they are interested in a more in-depth understanding of the faith, engaging them in a deeper dialogue is well worth the effort. We recommend setting up a regular meeting time (weekly is best) for discussion and study. It is best if there are at least three people: the leader, an apprentice, and the seeker (who is trying to figure out what he or she believes). It is best, as Jesus and Paul showed us, to bring others with you to learn from how you lead others. This is a context that allows for intimacy, openness, and impact. Often it's best if both a discussion leader and an apprentice leader guide the study (again, the leader is also discipling the apprentice). These two could be meeting with one to three non-Christians in a Transparent Context setting.

At our church we've developed different types of material for Christians to use specifically for engagement with non-Christian friends, family, neighbors, or coworkers in the Transparent Context. Each week people can go through a study like *Discovery Bible Studies,* which involve no preparation, or our more in-depth *Foundation's* material, in which participants go through the material at home and then come together to open their Bibles and talk about it, using prepared questions as a guide.

We take to heart the reality that the simple gospel message still requires an understanding of the broader story of the Bible, for Jesus died "according to scripture" (1 Cor. 15:4). This broader story is becoming less and less well known yet more and more important in a postmodern culture. In the ancient church, people often took a year or more of study before they made the commitment to be baptized. We're not saying that this amount of time is always necessary—people were baptized in the book of Acts immediately after hearing the gospel message for the first time, and the same thing happens today. But that is not the best way for many people, especially in a post-Christian context where basic assumptions about the Bible are no longer held.

Many nonbelievers need an intimate environment where they can learn, ask questions, and discover. They need time to process what it means to truly trust and follow Jesus. With the right material, the Transparent Context can help you to develop a solid friendship that leads to the deeper foundation of a relationship with Christ.

MINISTRY LEADERSHIP DEVELOPMENT

We've emphasized the role of the Transparent Context in developing ministry leaders in a local church. We teach our leaders to develop apprentice leaders in a church context as God leads them to servant-hearted Christians who fit our AFTR (AFTeR Jesus) leadership development or apprentice profile.[60]

- *Available.* They make themselves available for the things of God. It's not that they are less busy than other people but that they prioritize the things of God and make time for them (and him!).
- *Faithful.* They are faithful to the church or community. They consistently follow through and function as they have been asked or according to expectations.
- *Teachable.* They are receptive to guidance and instruction. They are humble in spirit and want to learn new things.

- *Reliable.* They have demonstrated a trustworthy character and consistently do what is asked.

Leadership development, as much as possible, should be based on the dynamics of the Transparent Context described earlier (intimacy, openness, and impact). Out of that framework, we recommend a formula similar to that promoted by Dave Ferguson and Jon Ferguson in their book *Exponential: How You and Your Friends Can Start a Missional Church Movement.*[61] This leadership apprentice model can be replicated in every ministry in a church, from hospital visitation to children's ministry to the role of the senior pastor (training an associate or church planter).

- I do. You watch. We talk.
- I do. You help. We talk.
- You do. I help. We talk.
- You do. I watch. We talk.
- You do. Someone else watches.

Earlier I mentioned a staff member at my church. His development in student ministry followed this pattern in various ways. For example, one of the theological values and beliefs of our church is that people give their hearts, by faith, to Jesus at the point of conversion through baptism by immersion. Our process sets people up with a covenant commitment where they not only call on Jesus to forgive their sins, but we help them to fully commit to discipleship from the beginning. When our student minister first started, he didn't have much experience working with students and parents from non-Christian families in making these decisions. So the first time a student wanted to commit her life to Christ this way, both he and I met with the young woman and her mother. I modeled for him how to handle things (including an extensive debriefing meeting afterward).

The next time I watched as he handled the meeting with a student, and I offered just a few pieces of advice with a shorter debriefing afterward. Before long he was on his own. Now he regularly takes people through the preparation process before they are baptized. The "do/watch/talk" model works in any kind of situation where one leader is training an emerging leader how to do something. It is typically very practical and creates a healthy leadership development process for tactical matters in which practice and proficiency make all the difference for emerging leaders.

A STRUGGLE FOR TRANSPARENCY

In his book *Scary Close*, Donald Miller describes his journey toward marriage as "dropping the act and finding true intimacy."[62] For many years he had trouble being genuine and vulnerable with others, and this reality hindered many of his close relationships. Miller married at the age of forty-two, and he says the main struggle he encountered in marriage was allowing himself to be vulnerable with his wife. He found that he could be authentic typing on the computer in a room by himself, writing books like *Blue Like Jazz* and *A Million Miles in a Thousand Years*, but being open and real while face-to-face with people was hard for him.

Not surprisingly, it's a challenge for many of us. When Miller realized that intimate relationships are *supposed* to be hard work, he decided he wasn't bad at relationships after all, just somewhat lazy. The analogy he uses now is that building a relationship is like training for a marathon, or sowing and harvesting a crop. It takes a lot of hard work, but it pays off over time.

The Transparent Context is like that. Relationships are hard work. Count on it! It takes time and patience to develop this level of intimacy with others, but it's worth it. It is one of the primary means through which the Holy Spirit changes lives today.

GETTING STARTED

1. Transparent Context groups are easy to start and flexible—so how can you jump into one? They can be started quickly as an add-on in a traditional church, or they can be developed with little supervision in a church plant.

2. What will you do in your group? (If you are looking for good material to guide you, see the following bibliography.)

3. (For church leaders:) If you have a good small group ministry, encourage men and women to subdivide into smaller, same-gender groups from the small group. Some groups will alternate—same-gender groups meet every even week and the mixed group meets every odd week.

4. Practically, I've noticed that men often love to meet for discipleship groups in the Transparent Context early in the morning before work. Women often prefer a night gathering, especially if child care is an issue.

ADDITIONAL RESOURCES FOR THE TRANSPARENT CONTEXT

Cobble, Tara-Leigh. *Mile Deep: A Practical Guide to Discipleship Groups.* Shrinking Music Publishing, 2014.

Cole, Neil. *Cultivating a Life for God: Multiplying Disciples through Life Transformation Groups.* Signal Hill, CA: CMA Resources, 2014.

Gallaty, Robby, and Randall Collins. *Growing Up: How to Be a Disciple Who Makes Disciples.* Bloomington, IN: CrossBooks, 2013.

Harrington, Bobby. *Foundations: The Storyline of the Real Jesus.* discipleship.org.

McNaughton, Daniel, and Bryan Koch. *Follow: Learning to Follow Jesus.* Spring City, PA: Morning Joy Media, 2010.

Pope, Randy. *Insourcing: Bringing Discipleship back to the Local Church.* Grand Rapids: Zondervan, 2013.

Buehring, David. *The Jesus Blueprint: Rediscovering His Original Plan for Changing the World.* Oviedo, FL: Higher Life Publishing, 2012.

Chapter Twelve

GOD SPEAKS TO YOU ALONE

Understanding the Divine Context

Key Principle: In the Divine Context, we are alone with God, and through the Holy Spirit we learn about our identity and destiny and are immersed in the truth.

DIVINE

Shortly after I (Bobby) became a Christian, I developed a habit of going off to a remote place for a day or two at a time to hear the voice of God. I don't remember anyone ever telling me to do this. It was something I sensed God leading me to do so that I could clearly hear his voice.

I remember one occasion very distinctly. I arranged to go to a remote hotel nestled in the mountains near Banff, Alberta, about an hour and a half from where we lived. Banff is a beautiful mountain resort area, one of the most stunning places in the world. It's easy to think that you will hear from God in that kind of setting.

At the time, I was struggling with some problems I was having with the church my wife and I were attending. I was not in ministry, because I was working at my dad's trucking company. And I was having trouble with several people in the church, and I had a certain disdain for one man in particular. I expected that on this retreat God would give me the green light to leave the church. I just needed to go away, pray, read my Bible and meditate, and God would give me that sense of clarity I needed to leave.

But that's not how it worked. On the second day something strange happened. I had a clear sense that God wanted me to look at things in a different way. God didn't seem to care about my complaints. I was getting a strong sense that he wanted me to face a fundamentally more important question: Did I love these people, and did I love the man I was struggling with in particular?

I came away from that time transformed with a fresh commitment not only to love those people but to show genuine love in particular to the man who was bothering me. As soon as I got back, we ran into each other. I knew money was tight for him, so I offered to give him some cash as a gift. To my surprise, he thanked me and took the money! After that, our relationship changed significantly, and I never had that struggle with him again.

We want to mention up front that God is discipling us in all of the contexts. All five are, in a true sense, Divine Contexts. But a central discipling place for all of life is the relational space we have with God, where he disciples us directly. God uses people, yes. But he often does his work apart from direct interaction with other people. We place the Divine Context at the center of life change because it is here that each person experiences the immediate presence of the Spirit of God. Again, this is not to minimize our need for other layers of discipleship. They are important to holistic spiritual growth, but without the vital connection we have to God through the Holy Spirit, authentic transformation will not happen. There are times when we are left alone with God, and in this place, we are known for who we really are.

> **God uses people, yes. But he often does his work apart from direct interaction with other people.**

THE DIVINE CONTEXT

The Divine Context is how we describe our direct interaction with God himself, apart from other people, as we respond to the gentle yet distinct promptings of the Holy Spirit. The focus here shifts from relationships with others to solitude with God as he encounters us in our inner world. At this level, we are laid bare before him, and he opens himself to us. We come face-to-face with our true selves.

The Divine Context of discipleship gives us the capacity to engage fully in the other contexts. Without a one-on-one friendship with God, we have nothing of substance upon which to build our lives and relationships. The Divine Context is often thought of as the place where we engage in spiritual disciplines or habits.

Throughout the centuries Christian leaders have pointed to this context as an essential environment for true spiritual growth and empowerment for living a Christian life of vitality. While we'll touch on a few of the key characteristics and outcomes of this context, several classic and contemporary authors have created a significant body of literature that we recommend.[63]

> **Without a one-on-one friendship with God, we have nothing of substance upon which to build our lives and relationships.**

Jesus in the Divine Context

Jesus offers us the primary model for how to be alone with the Father and gain strength from that time with him. Nowhere do we see this connection more explicitly than during Jesus' conversation with his disciples the week before his death. In anticipation of his trial and the Passion to come, Jesus told his disciples, "Behold, the hour is coming, indeed it has come, when you will be scattered, each to his own home, and will leave me alone" (John 16:32 ESV). Jesus was facing his most vulnerable moment on earth, when he would be tried and executed, and his best friends abandoned him. But he didn't remain in a state of despair because he knew that even apart from all human relationships, he was never actually alone. He told his disciples, "You will . . . leave me alone. Yet I am not alone, for the Father is with me" (John 16:32 ESV).

Jesus' entire life, as recorded in the Gospels, shows the regular practice of spiritual habits (aka "spiritual disciplines") in the Divine Context. He demonstrated the "how–to" of the disciplines, as well as the power of a close relationship with God. Here are some of the habits Jesus practiced:

- *Private prayer.* He withdrew to lonely places to pray in private (Luke 5:16).

- *Extended prayer.* He spent extended periods of time in prayer before he chose the twelve disciples and before his death (Luke 6:12; 22:41).

- *Fasting.* He fasted for forty days and nights at the beginning of his public ministry (Luke 4:1–13).

- *Study of Scripture.* He engaged with Scripture so that by the age of twelve he knew and understood enough to converse with scholars at the temple (Luke 2:41–50), and by the age of thirty he had memorized many passages, as revealed during the temptations (Luke 4:1–13).

- *Retreat.* He withdrew from the public after he found out that John the Baptist had been executed (Matt. 14:13–15).

- *Celebration.* He attended feasts and parties (e.g., John 2:1–10).

- *Giving.* He made a habit of giving to the poor, which is why the Twelve suspected he might have commanded Judas to give money away (John 13:29).

- *Secrecy.* Several times after Jesus healed someone, he asked them not to tell anyone. He practiced secrecy (e.g., Mark 7:36).

If we could make just one comment to Christians living in our culture today, it would be that God does not leave you alone. The Divine Context is the place where he is the most immanent, the closest to you. Some of the most important moments of transformation in your life, as you mature in discipleship, will be experiences alone with the Lord. Like Jesus, you are alone physically during these times, but not relationally or spiritually, because God is with you. Sometimes these moments of solitude with God are places of testing, yet they also can be very rewarding.

Take Jesus' temptation in the wilderness, for example (Luke 4:1–13). He was led by the Holy Spirit into the desert to be alone with God for forty days. In the desert, without other people around, God wanted Jesus to face his enemy, Satan. God designed this place to be the crucible of spiritual preparation for his Son. Jesus proved his faithfulness to God, his Father, by rebuking Satan and rejecting the temptations of his enemy.

The desert was not a place of spiritual weakness for Jesus—quite the opposite. Jesus exercised his spiritual muscles and *grew* through the physical and psychological challenges of fasting and solitude. We know he was not alone but was anointed and led by the Holy Spirit. He cited this passage to Satan, his accuser: "Man shall not live on bread alone, but on every word that comes from the mouth of God" (Matt. 4:4). We see here that Jesus was listening to his Father, learning to hear from God in the desert, and this time prepared him for his later ministry among the crowds after his public ministry began. What Jesus practiced in secret became habit in public.

In the same way that Jesus made a habit of getting away to pray and hear from God, our bodies need to "learn" these habits as well. Dallas Willard puts it this way:

> Somewhat ironically, perhaps, all of the "spiritual" disciplines are, or essentially involve, bodily behaviors. But really, that makes perfect sense. For the body is the first field of energy beyond our thoughts that we have direction over, and all else we influence is due to our power over it. Moreover, it is the chief repository of the wrong habits that we must set aside, as well as the place where new habits are to be instituted. We are, within limits, able to command it to do things that will transform our habits—especially the inner habits of thought and feeling—and so enable us to do things not now in our power.[64]

When my son and I visited Israel for the first time, the tour guide showed us the place where, according to tradition, Jesus in Mark 1:35 withdrew to be alone to pray. Jesus' place of prayer now exists as a stone cutout in the side of a grassy hill about six feet tall, fifteen feet wide, and ten feet deep on the northern shore of the Sea of Galilee, near Capernaum.

Since we were there, my son and I decided to do what Jesus did and get up before sunrise while we were staying at a hotel near the area.

Jesus made a habit of getting away to pray and hear from God.

The next day we woke up at 5:00 a.m., thinking the sky would still be dark. But the sun was already shining at that time. So the next night we went to bed, wanting to do *exactly* what Jesus had done, and woke up "while it was still dark" the following morning at 4:00 a.m. This time it was still dark out and we had some time to hike to Jesus' place of prayer before the sun came up. When we got to that small stone cutout on the hill, we saw the sky, dark before sunrise, and we made space

196 Discipleship That Fits

in our hearts to hear from God. Besides the lapping of the waves, the silence of the morning filled us with peace as we prayed where Jesus had prayed two thousand years ago. We were together, father and son, and far from being a distraction, this closeness gave us a vision for how Jesus prioritized and cultivated his relationship with his own heavenly Father. We both understood that Jesus made time for that essential relationship, even at the cost of a few hours of sleep.

The Divine Context in the Old Testament

In addition to the model we see in the life of Jesus, we think of King David, the archetypal king of the Old Testament. David also learned how to draw strength from spending time alone with God. Several of the psalms highlight times of deep disappointment and despair in David's life. We also read of a time when he fled his homeland for a foreign land. Six hundred fighting men were with him as he went on raids. Yet one day when he came home with his men, he found that his new home had been burned down and his family taken captive. He and his men wept loudly to the point of exhaustion. Then, to make matters worse, his troops turned on him and thought about stoning him. Everyone was bitter and upset, and his friends wanted to harm him. "But," the Bible tells us, "David found strength in the LORD his God" (1 Sam. 30:6).

Each of us needs to be prepared for moments like this, when everyone we know and love deserts us or even turns on us, and all we can do is look to God for help. Our crisis may not be as dramatic as David's, but we all will face situations where we feel abandoned and alone in our lives. The journey of being a disciple of Jesus always takes us on the Via Dolorosa, the path of suffering that leads to the cross. And in one fashion or another, we must learn how to walk it with God, who never leaves us alone.

These moments are precious. We would never plan them or seek them, but when they come, they are opportunities for immense spiritual growth. Consider what happened with David after this crisis moment. He went on to defeat his enemies, recover all that was taken from his city as spoil, and rescue his family (1 Sam. 30:16–20). David won that battle, but imagine if he had given in to despair—in that case, he may not have come away in victory.

David developed a very personal, intimate relationship with God during years alone in the fields where he was shepherding his father's sheep. Later, as a grown man, he knew how to dialogue with God in an honest and life-giving way. God heard him, and David gained strength. Had David not developed this relationship with the Lord before this crisis moment, his first response may not have been to turn to God. But because he had trained himself to look to God as his refuge and strength, he turned fully to God in hope, and it was a pivotal moment in the history of the nation, his family, and his men.

Many other examples from biblical and church history show us how the Divine Context is central to discipleship. Consider studying the life of one or two of the following people, taking note of how they related to God and how God spoke to them in turn:

- Adam and Eve (Gen. 3:8)
- Noah (Gen. 6:13–21)
- Abraham (Gen. 12:1–3)
- Jonah (Jonah 1:1)
- Job (Job 40:1)
- Joseph (Gen. 40:8)
- Daniel (Dan. 6:10)
- Other prophets: Isaiah, Jeremiah, and Ezekiel (Isa. 6:8; Jer. 1:2; Ezek. 1:1)

The Divine Context in the New Testament

The Divine Context is evident in the New Testament as well, and not only in the life of Jesus. The apostle Paul also spent at least three years in a desert region (Gal. 1:15–17). Soon after his conversion, Paul went into the Arabian Desert and to Damascus, where he did not consult anyone but waited to meet the apostles. Some scholars believe that this is where Jesus personally discipled Paul through spiritual experiences. Whether or not Paul was actually alone in the desert (or he interacted with other Jews in the area), he seems to have developed an intimate relationship with God during those years.

Perhaps Paul was studying the Hebrew Bible and relearning how to read the Scriptures through a Jesus-centered lens. Or maybe he simply needed time to process his new change of heart after years of persecuting Christians. God ministered to Paul as an individual, changing him forever. Paul later said, "I no longer live, but Christ lives in me. The life I live in the body, I live by faith in the Son of God, who loved me and gave himself for me" (Gal. 2:20). This passage, along with many others in his letters, reveals that Paul cultivated a personal relationship with God, and that gave him power to face imprisonment later on in life (Acts 16:23; 20:23; 27:42). Paul learned, as we all must, the spiritual discipline of being alone with God.

As with anything in life, growth in spiritual practices and disciplines comes only with time and training. So why do we think we can grow up spiritually without any effort? Perhaps the reason lies in the fact that we live in a consumeristic, fast-food

As with anything in life, growth in spiritual practices and disciplines comes only with time and training.

culture, but that's not how spiritual growth happens. To be clear, when we speak of exerting effort, we are not thinking of earning favor with God or merit before him. The Bible is clear that we must exert real effort to mature in Christ, though this effort is evidence of God's saving grace at work in our life. Still, this effort is required of all who follow Christ. Dallas Willard describes the importance of the body in Divine Context discipleship by referring to a New Testament letter written by Paul to Timothy:

> The context in which Paul uses the words "exercise unto godliness" is an intensely practical one. He is telling Timothy, his son in the faith, how to succeed in leading God's people. In speaking of exercise or training he uses the term *gumnaze*, from which we get our term "gymnasium." Instead of spending time dwelling on godless myths and legends, Paul tells his young friend, he is to be at work in the "spiritual gymnasium": "Train (*gumnaze*) yourself unto godliness; for while bodily training (*gumnasia*) is of some value, godliness is of value in every way, as it holds promise for the present life and also for the life to come" (1 Tim. 4:7–8, RSV).[65]

In addition to Paul, John of Patmos is another New Testament example of discipleship in the Divine Context. He was exiled to the arid island of Patmos, which lies off the coast of modern-day Turkey (then called Asia Minor). While scholars believe other exiles may have lived in this place, we have no indication that John had interactions with anyone else during this time.

In the context of a lonely and desolate island in the middle of the sea, God spoke some of the most powerful (and beautiful) words on record. He delivered the visions of the book of Revelation to John on Patmos. John was in the Spirit on the Lord's Day, and he saw apocalyptic visions and heard oracles from heaven. Just as God spoke to Elijah with a whisper in the silence of Mount Carmel, so he spoke to John in the quiet of Patmos. God speaks loudest when we are alone, and it is every disciple's responsibility to make space for silence in order to listen well to his words.

GOALS FOR DISCIPLESHIP IN THE DIVINE CONTEXT

Certain aspects of discipleship can be fully developed only within the Divine Context. We have identified three goals for our relationship alone with God: *identity*, *destiny*, and *truth*.

Goal 1: Identity

Recalling Jesus' temptation in the desert, one of the primary challenges he faced was a question of identity. Three times he was tempted, and two times the tempter began with the words, "If you are the Son of God . . ." (Luke 4:3, 9). While Jesus faced trials of power, sustenance, and survival, a common theme was who he was, the Son of God. Satan was challenging his identity.

Just as Satan tempted Jesus, the Accuser tempts us in many ways, but his most challenging attack is against our identity as children of God. It is a major threat, because it concerns our status before God, whether we are truly his or not. Identity is part of everyone's personality, but followers of Jesus have unique identities as beloved children of God.

What's more, God loves you in particular. He has given you a unique identity in addition to calling you his child. In a funny way, it's like the words of Dr. Seuss, "Today you are You, that is truer than true. There is no one alive who is Youer than You." God forms our identity in our aloneness more than in any other relational context, it seems, because when we are alone we can filter out all the identities the world puts on us and truly listen to God.

> **The Accuser tempts us in many ways, but his most challenging attack is against our identity as children of God.**

If we're not careful, we allow Satan more space than we allow God to speak into our hearts when we are alone. We easily look for Satan behind every bush so we can claim, "I was being tempted, and that's why I sinned!" While sometimes we are tempted by Satan or demons, other times it is simply our own sin that tempts us. Jack Deere, in his book *Surprised by the Power of the Spirit*, corrects this false emphasis.[66] He says that if we find Satan at work in so many ways in our lives, how much more active is the Holy Spirit in our lives!

From beginning to end, God is forming us into mature disciples. In Ephesians 2:1–6 Paul says that we used to live in sin when we followed "the spirit that is now at work in the sons of disobedience." He goes on to say, "But God, being rich in mercy, because of the great love with which he loved us, even when we were dead in our trespasses, made us alive together with Christ" (ESV). So from the beginning God makes us alive, and Jesus promises to carry his disciples through to the end, even as we teach others to follow him. He said to his disciples in the Great Commission, "Surely I am with you always, to the very end of the age" (Matt. 28:20).

Goal 2: Destiny

Similar to identity, God-given destiny is the work of the Holy Spirit inside a person's heart, apart from the direct influence of others. Destiny is about God's call on your life. It is about following God's guidance into the destiny or ministry work to which he has called you.

When you were seven years old, what did you want to be when you grew up? Alex asked this question on Facebook and received hundreds of answers—some of them very funny! Here are a few of the more "unique" answers:

- "An international jewel thief—we clearly watched too many Pink Panther movies at my house!"

- "An army nurse, so I could save a soldier's life and he'd marry me. Or a ballerina, or private detective. I wasn't putting all my eggs in one basket."

- "Playboy bunny!! (I wanted the costume—had no idea what the role meant!!)"

- "Until I learned the downside of it, I wanted to be a Bank Robber because I assumed they made lots of money. I distinctly remember telling my parents about my career goals, and how it felt to have the rug pulled out from under me. Dream killers."

The sense of destiny that you have for your life holds tremendous power. It helps give you direction and purpose and can be highly motivating. It is a special gift God has given you because he has designed you to live a life that truly matters.[67]

Our God is the God who dreamed you up—which makes you the fulfillment of his dream. Wow! But here's the thing: too often we allow the big dream to be overtaken by the clamor of the American dream. Not that living in a welcoming home or driving a comfortable car is wrong, but too often we allow those things to become *the* dream.

Here's where we go back to basics and recognize the difference between the American dream and the kingdom dream. The former is essentially about me (and, as an extension of my ego, my family), whereas the latter is essentially about others. It is about investing in others in ways that could never be repaid. God's dream in you is expressed as you help the dreams of others to be expressed.

> The dream is not about you—it is about your following Jesus and changing the world, one person at a time, in the name of Jesus.

You see, the dream is not about you—it is about your following Jesus and changing the world, one person at a time, in the name of Jesus. It is about impacting every area of culture and society as we help others move into their God-given identity, purpose, and destiny.

But to do that with genuine impact, we must allow Jesus to have a close hand on our own hearts. Humans tend to place the highest value on skills and competency, whereas Jesus places the highest value on heart and character. If you want to be a world changer, Jesus must be radically shaping your character.

Goal 3: Truth

The third goal of spending time alone with God is knowing God's truth. This can refer to factual knowledge, of course, but it means more than just that. Knowing the truth means having a relational knowledge of truth— knowing truth in such a way that it shapes who you are. It forms your character, defines your desires, and influences your choices. A common definition of character is "who you are when no one is looking." Truth at work in your character, your desires, and your will is your identity in action, and it cannot be faked. Instead, this work of truth must be carried out in your heart by God. These lessons are often painful at first but rewarding in the end. That's why Paul says in Romans, "We rejoice in our sufferings, knowing that suffering produces endurance, and endurance produces character, and character produces hope" (5:3–4 ESV).

I (Bobby) commonly find that it is only when I am alone with God and fully present before him that the Holy Spirit leads me to consider who I am on the inside. Often I am too preoccupied with busyness, tasks, and other activities to hear God. That's why I love to take long prayer walks in the morning (or late at night) or, even better, to schedule time to go away for private spiritual retreats. Here is what invariably happens as God reveals his truth to me:

- *I get my mind and spirit right.* I first have to clear my mind and settle my spirit down through the words of Scripture. Because of the way I'm wired, I have a hard time calming my spirit unless I first engage with God in his Word. Sometimes spiritual music will help me to do that or just being alone with God in nature. But almost always, it is reading the Bible.

- *I call out to God.* Once my mind and spirit are settled in the presence of God, I call out to him. I typically use a prayer model, like the Lord's Prayer, as an outline. And then I talk about the things that have been on my mind or ask the Lord to guide my thoughts.

- *I wait patiently for God's guidance.* I sense God leading me to a spiritual truth related to what I'm talking to him about (sometimes he takes my mind in new directions). It is gentle nudging and subtle guidance.

- *I remain open to God's Spirit.* The place that God takes me typically ends up being a place of realization about something that I missed or was lacking. Sometimes it involves a strong sense of affirmation; many times it involves a change of heart on my part.

- *I accept his truth.* The new awareness comes to me with a sense of truth—it is self-authenticating. It is not forced or pressured. It is just the voice of God speaking into my spirit and guiding my thoughts.

- *I move forward in confidence.* Through this process I gain a clear sense of assurance about God's direction or affirmation or call to repentance in my life; then I move into his guidance with confidence.

- *I look for corroboration.* Wise Christians who are experienced in the spiritual life have taught me that when God's Spirit speaks, his guidance usually is validated by the circumstances of life, the teachings of the Bible, and especially the counsel of godly leaders. The bigger the sense of change in our lives, the more important it is to look for corroboration from these other modes of God's leading. Dallas Willard has some profoundly helpful material that elaborates on these matters. (See his *Hearing God: Developing a Conversational Relationship with God.*[68])

Willard warns that when you go into these times of solitude, you must make as clear as possible to those with whom you are in regular relationship why you are doing it. That way they support you rather than resent you during these times.

God is the Master Teacher, and he works well with those who make space in their lives for him. In addition to seeking direction or reconnecting relationally with God, you may choose to set apart a period of solitude and separation to address certain sins in your life. This process typically requires a combination of several spiritual habits and practices to help you achieve your goal. The 12-Step movement, drawing upon Christian spiritual practices, has benefited many people in this way. Often this approach combines the Personal Context (an extended group) and the Transparent Context (a one-on-one relationship with a sponsor) with the Divine Context (times of solitude) to help those struggling to find freedom from their addiction. I'm particularly pleased to see a number of churches adopting Celebrate Recovery as an explicit Christian foundation for the 12 Steps and various spiritual practices.

God is the Master Teacher, and he works well with those who make space in their lives for him.

LEARNING GOD'S LOVE LANGUAGE

The first step in moving closer to God is to recognize that you need an intimate relationship with him. The Bible says, "Come near to God and he will come near to you" (James 4:8). He is relational by nature; he is not something to know about but a person to know deeply. The spiritual practices we've described are another way of describing God's love language. In other words, if you want to connect with God, you can do it your way with little success; but if you come near to him in the ways he has revealed throughout history, especially through his Son, Jesus, you will find joy in connecting with him. As disciples of Jesus, we cannot be greater than him, but we can be like him! And he knew God deeply.

In the next chapter we'll take what we have described in theory here and apply it to real life. The spiritual practices of Jesus, David, and many other biblical figures may seem unattainable, but God offers his intimate fellowship to everyone who believes in Jesus. He wants to speak identity into your life and build your character to be like his. As you grow in grace and truth, you will begin to form godly dreams for the kingdom, out of which God will bless the world through you. What a beautiful journey to be on!

Chapter Thirteen

THE EMPOWERING PRESENCE

Discipleship in the Divine Context

> **Key Application:** Create and sustain a culture in the church that emphasizes alone time with God and spiritual disciplines as part of the normal Christian life.

As a church leadership team, we decided we weren't just going to talk about the importance of being in the Bible and praying daily. We were going to embark on an earnest effort to get everybody in the church practicing some of the basic spiritual habits on a daily basis.

We knew that people needed help. Most had never been discipled in how to develop an inner life. They had heard people talk about it but needed someone to show them how to do it. So, we thought, let's keep it simple, easy to do, and then ask everyone to join us.

So we created a journal and an app. People could choose to use one or both. We provided the sermon outlines and small group questions for the week, two fairly common practices, but then took it one step farther by furnishing daily readings and teaching a reflection and prayer method that everyone could easily follow. It required a ten-minute commitment every day.

Soon lots of people were reading their Bibles every day, reflecting on how what they read applied to their lives, and praying earnestly. We had equipped everyone in the basic practices of Divine Context discipleship and knew that God was going to use these practices to help people trust and follow Jesus.

Discipleship in the Divine Context is God's direct interaction with you through his Holy Spirit. We've described why engagement in this context is important; now we'll explore how it can work in everyday life.

When you tune in to God's ongoing work in your heart, all of your other relationships will be affected by your movement toward God and toward grace. While you can hide major sin or minor blunders from others at various levels, there's no hiding with God! Consider the words of 1 John 1:6–9: "If we claim to have fellowship with him and yet walk in the darkness, we lie and do not live out the truth. But if we walk in the light, as he is in the light, we have fellowship with one another, and the blood of Jesus, his Son, purifies us from all sin. If we claim to be without sin, we deceive ourselves and the truth is not in us. If we confess our sins, he is faithful and just and will forgive us our sins and purify us from all unrighteousness."

> When you tune in to God's ongoing work in your heart, all of your other relationships will be affected by your movement toward God and toward grace.

You cannot hide from the truth. That simple reality is both the power to change and the challenge of change at the level of divine discipleship.

If you think you are in control in the Divine Context, you are in for a shock! God's kingdom means that he is reigning as king. And God wants to take over every corner of your home, every inch of your skin, and every space in your heart—he wants it all! The reason he wants everything under his control is because it is already his. He made you and loves you and knows what's best for you. His kingship calls you to make a willful surrender (sometimes called repentance); though it is painful at first, in the end it brings renewal and vitality to every part of your life. Jesus said, "I came that they may have life and have it abundantly" (John 10:10 ESV).

DISCIPLESHIP IN THE DIVINE CONTEXT

The most important takeaway from the Bible stories in the previous chapter is that God himself personally taught and discipled his people. God gave David strength for battle and taught him how to gain victory over his enemies. God taught Paul and John about his character so they could teach others about him. And God made Jesus to grow in wisdom and stature (Luke 2:40), and Jesus "learned obedience from what he suffered" (Heb. 5:8).

How does divine discipleship work, though, for us as followers of Jesus today? You might be saying to yourself, I'm not a king like David, or an apostle like Paul, or the Son of God like Jesus, so does this teaching apply to me as well? Most certainly it does.

We can look back over two thousand years of church history to see how Christians have returned, time after time, to several tried and true practices that make room for us to listen to God. These disciplines include silence, solitude, giving to the poor, fasting, prayer, Scripture reading, and meditation. They even encompass some less commonly discussed practices such as celebration, secrecy, and journaling. Many practices are important to cultivate so that we fully mature as disciples, but we want to focus on four core practices that provide the foundation for the other practices.

We also want to note that leaders are responsible for modeling to other Christians how to grow as a disciple through spiritual practices. This kind of modeling begins and ends with a leader's personal integrity—not that you must have a flawless track record in the spiritual disciplines, but it's true that you can take people only as far as you have gone in your walk with God. As a leader, then, you will need to remain open to growth, alongside others, by continually going deeper in your own relationship with God. You may settle into a steady rhythm with God at times, but you can never settle for staying where you were at yesterday. As the saying goes, "You can't teach what you don't know, and you can't lead where you won't go."

As you continue to develop your own intimacy with God, you can gently lead others with patience as they learn the basics. Rehearsing the basics yourself is always beneficial, and what better way to do so than by simply practicing the disciplines with those you disciple and lead!

- If you want to teach someone to pray, pray with them.
- If they've never fasted before, invite them to join you in some form of fasting.
- If they need to learn to read the Word, read Scripture with them.
- If they don't know how to minister to the poor, involve them in an outreach effort.

They will learn as they go, and by going with you, they will learn well the essential lessons you've already learned. In this way, everyone you disciple will be able to stand on your shoulders and reach higher in coming generations. Who knows what God has in store for them in the future!

Let's review in more detail the four core practices for growing as a disciple in the Divine Context.

Practice 1: Prayer

We begin with prayer because it is among the few disciplines that Jesus took for granted among his disciples. He said to them, "When you pray . . ." He assumed that they were praying people and that they just needed direction on how to pray.

Prayer is something that Jesus says we should do alone, though it is appropriate in other more public contexts as well. Jesus told his disciples, "When you pray, do not be like the hypocrites. . . . But when you pray, go into your room, close the door and pray to your Father, who is unseen. Then your Father, who sees what is done in secret, will reward you" (Matt. 6:5–6).

Carving out a specific time to pray in secret every day will be a "means of grace" from God, as John Wesley called the disciplines and other Christian practices. Prayer, along with the other means of grace, will breathe life into every pore of your body and bring vitality to every aspect of your life. The goal is not to compartmentalize your life into two categories: prayer time and the rest of life. The goal is that your focused times of prayer will spill into all your everyday events and that you'll even pray spontaneously! As Paul said, "In every situation, by prayer and petition, with thanksgiving, present your requests to God" (Phil. 4:6).

Your focused times of prayer will spill into all your everyday events.

As I mentioned at the beginning of this chapter, our church leadership team decided to help our members develop some basic and unified daily spiritual practices. So we created a Bible-reading and prayer journal that integrates Scripture and prayer; it's a simple way to start (or restart) a daily routine of spending time in the Word before God. This is more than just reading, since we can't hide our true selves from God. We read Scripture, and it reads us.

A prayer journal is a place where you can lay your heart bare before our Father in heaven, telling him everything you are thinking. He already knows your secret thoughts and deepest longings and will honor you for your openness before him.

A journal also gives you a way to chronicle the experiences that you and Jesus have together in God's Word. A journal like the one we've created will help you to (1) read the Bible daily and (2) pray daily. It includes prompts encouraging you to pray, examine your life, interact with others, and take notes on what Jesus is saying to you through the daily readings and Sunday morning teachings.

There are many great approaches to journaling. We use the SOAP journaling method developed by pastor Wayne Cordeiro.[69] We encourage this method because it's simple and easy to remember: SOAP stands for Scripture, Observation, Application, and Prayer. It's a straightforward way to process what you are learning in Scripture.

First, you get your Bible, a journal, and something to write with. Then you find a quiet, distraction-free place. You open your Bible to today's reading and underline or highlight any verses that grab your attention or speak to your life circumstances.

- *Scripture.* Start by writing out the verse or verses you've highlighted. It's amazing what happens when you slow down and write the Word of God with your own hand!

- *Observation.* Next, think about the meaning of the Scripture, including anything that especially stood out to you. Always be sure to read the passage in context. Here are some questions to consider: Who is the author? Who is the audience? What does this text reveal about God? What does it reveal about human nature?

- *Application.* Get personal here. If you took the Scripture you wrote down seriously, what about your life would change? How does this passage change the way you view God? How will it affect the way you treat others?

- *Prayer.* Finally, write out a prayer to God based on what you just learned and ask him to help you apply these truths to your life.

Practice 2: Fasting

In addition to prayer, Jesus also assumed his disciples would regularly fast from food for defined periods of time. He said, "When you fast, do not look gloomy like the hypocrites. . . . But when you fast, anoint your head and wash your face. . . . And your Father who sees in secret will reward you" (Matt. 6:16 ESV).

We mention fasting from food here not because it's easy, but because Jesus mentions it as one of the three common ways to connect with God. And it's an important way that saints throughout history have expressed deep devotion to God, adopting this practice from the Bible, which records how people fasted from food during times of intense transition, sadness, or repentance. By withholding physical nutrients from your body for a certain period of time, you enable a special focus on the nourishment that comes from God's voice. It's not magic; it's simply a practical way to connect with God.

Through the words of Jesus in Matthew 6, God is inviting you to know him in deeper ways not only by praying but by using your body to express prayers of deep longing.

Practice 3: Giving to the Poor

The third act of righteousness that Jesus assumes his disciples will practice, in addition to prayer and fasting, is giving to the poor. "When you give to the needy, do not let your left hand know what your right hand is doing, so that your giving may be in secret. Then your Father, who sees what is done in secret, will reward you" (Matt. 6:3–4). In our context we would add that this means more than just writing a check to a non-profit agency that serves the poor, or dropping off some old clothes at the Goodwill store. It involves personal interactions with the poor, something taken for granted in ancient times. If you're reading this book, it's likely you are financially able to serve the poor in a personal way.

We've included giving to the poor as a way to be discipled by God because throughout history God has often taught his people by asking them to *do* something. For example, Abraham's journey started with a simple command: "Go from your country, your people and your father's household to the land I will show you" (Gen. 12:1–3). The apostle Paul also discipled by command, giving Timothy simple instructions like, "Stay in Ephesus and appoint elders." Even Jesus told the rich young ruler simply, "Go, sell everything you have and give to the poor" (Mark 10:21). He didn't teach him where to sell his stuff or how much to sell it for or whether to discount his sofa. He simply said, "Sell it." Our point is that learning by doing is something God himself uses to teach us.

By simply doing what God asks us to do, or even what we think he might want, we learn new ways of thinking.

Alan Hirsch and Michael Frost articulate this simple principle in *The Faith of Leap*. They remind us that by simply doing what God asks us to do, or even what we think he might want, we learn new ways of thinking. And in the process our faith in God inevitably increases. They write, "Even knowing truths about God is not enough to save—the Pharisees had that all pinned down. No, we must actively risk ourselves to the truth that we believe is true, and this in turn involves staking our lives on the person and the promises of God."[70]

Prayer, fasting, and giving to the poor are all addressed by Jesus in his Sermon on the Mount (Matthew 5–7). Every command he gives can be traced back to one of the central themes in the sermon: developing a deep-rooted true righteousness, from the inside out.

Our advice to you in these matters is not complicated. We're saying simply, "Just do it." Whatever God is calling you to do to give your resources away, just do it. He will teach you how. Experience will come with time. And the experiences and counsel of others will help us, too, but nothing will teach you as well as just launching into these acts of righteousness and learning from God himself what the details look like.

Jesus told his disciples, "You may ask me for anything in my name, and I will do it" (John 14:14). "Just doing it" is a process of discovery and a journey of experiencing God, so don't worry about how it will work out in the end. Seek first God's kingdom and righteousness, and the main stuff you need to survive will be taken care of (Matt. 6:33). Take a step out of your comfort zone and learn what the leap of faith actually feels like! And the Bible promises that God will reward you, not necessarily financially but certainly with the greatest of treasures—his presence.

212 Discipleship That Fits

Practice 4: Personal Bible Reading

We add Bible reading here because it is a specific way of listening to God. Listening is different from merely reading, though, so we use the word "reading" carefully. There are many ways to read words on a page. When we read God's Word with the goal of listening to God, we allow it to affect our lives in all sorts of ways.

One way that Christians over the centuries have developed the skill of listening to God's voice is by meditating on Scripture as they read it. Dietrich Bonhoeffer instituted a practice of Scripture meditation among his students in the Confessional Church seminary that he helped found during Hitler's regime.[71] Even when they were eventually scattered across the country, Bonhoeffer, his students, and his friends would meditate on one passage from the Bible for thirty minutes every morning. They all chose the same reading schedule so they could think about the same passage every day. Each person would pick one word, one phrase, or one sentence and during a time of silence would focus their thoughts on a particular word from God.

What was unique was that those meditating were told to receive that Scripture as God's personal message to them. It was as if Jesus spoke it directly to them and it was as applicable now as it was then. This discipline, also practiced in a similar way by C. S. Lewis, was a constant source of strength and encouragement to those Christians who resisted the force of Nazism over Christianity. One of our goals as Christians is to be men and women who meditate on God's Word all day and even into the night. As the psalmist says, "Blessed is the one who does not walk in step with the wicked or stand in the way that sinners take or sit in the company of mockers, but whose delight is in the law of the LORD, and who meditates on his law day and night" (Ps. 1:1–2).

We've found that one of the most important disciplines for Christians to learn is reading the Word for themselves. In working with Cally Parkinson of the Willow Creek Association on the results of the REVEAL Study, I asked her what they had learned about the role of personal Bible study and how it impacts a person's growth. She summed up for me what they had learned after surveying more than 250,000 Christians and 1,500 churches. She said, "The single most important thing a church can do to help people to grow is to help them to engage with God in the Bible on a daily basis." For this reason, among many others, we feel that we cannot overstate the importance of developing a habit of reading the Bible every day and listening for God to speak to you as you read.

GETTING TO KNOW GOD

Our culture has a unique dilemma: we have lots of interactions with people but few true connections. For Christians, this is a double dilemma because we may deal with loneliness in our culture and yet also are called to withdraw from people on a regular basis to seek energy and wisdom from God. The solution, we believe, is in learning the difference between isolation and solitude.

Isolation is different from solitude. Those who enter into times of solitude do so with intent and purpose. Those in isolation, however, may not have chosen their circumstances. Or if they have chosen to be alone, the reason may be rooted in guilt or fear. Whatever the case, the isolation causes these individuals to become confused, lonely, or both.

A person who chooses to be alone in order to grow as a person through the disciplines associated with solitude is not isolated. And the difference is in the result. You can ask yourself, "Am I energized after being alone?" or "What did I gain by being alone?" Answering these questions will help you navigate the way to solitude with God. When you experience God in solitude, you will walk away stronger, ready to give yourself away to the world.

One of the best lessons we learn when practicing the spiritual disciplines is to approach God as a person, not as a means to an end. In other words, when we fast or pray, we don't always need an immediate, clear answer in order to accomplish our goal. Indeed, being close to God *is* the goal!

But if we are in a true and authentic relationship with God, we can ask for his gifts and answers to our prayers. As a parent loves to care for his child, God loves to care for us. But, again, we don't want to feel like we are trying to manipulate

> **One of the best lessons we learn when practicing the spiritual disciplines is to approach God as a person, not as a means to an end.**

God when we meet him in his Word or through prayer or fasting. We simply get God and a relationship with him. Whatever fruit comes from that relationship is fine at that point, because we know that we've truly connected with our Father.

Likewise, in prayer, we don't just want to talk about what we need from God. Instead, we focus on who God is and what he is doing in our lives, in our neighborhoods, and in the world. Just as much as we ask God for something, we simply express that we need him in our lives! That kind of relationship is built on companionship, and it's one we want to continue to cultivate.

GETTING STARTED

1. Develop a strong daily devotional habit and regular spiritual disciplines. Do an audit of your habits by recording them for a month and then sharing the results with a mature Christian friend, asking for their observations, encouragements, and suggestions for growth.

2. Take those you lead with you on spiritual retreats, and invite them to join you in specific seasons of fasting and prayer.

3. (For church leaders:) Create teaching series on these themes. Maybe provide journals to encourage the deeper spiritual life (for instance, as a church encourage everyone to journal through Lent).

4. Raise the bar: ask those you lead to be regularly accountable for their spiritual lives.

5. Fast and pray earnestly and regularly for revival in the church.

ADDITIONAL RESOURCES FOR THE DIVINE CONTEXT

Benner, David G. *Desiring God's Will: Aligning Our Hearts with the Heart of God*. Downers Grove, IL: InterVarsity Press, 2005.

Foster, Richard J. *Celebration of Discipline: The Path to Spiritual Growth*, 3rd ed. San Francisco: HarperSanFrancisco, 1998.

Nouwen, Henri J. M. *The Way of the Heart*. New York: Ballantine Books, 2003.

Ortberg, John. *The Life You've Always Wanted: Spiritual Disciplines for Ordinary People*, expanded ed. Grand Rapids: Zondervan, 2002.

Willard, Dallas. *The Spirit of the Disciplines: Understanding How God Changes Lives*. San Francisco: HarperSanFrancisco, 1990.

Chapter Fourteen

SOME OF YOUR QUESTIONS PREEMPTIVELY ANSWERED

Applying the Five Contexts

It is easy to think that the Church has a lot of different objects—education, building, missions, holding services. . . . Church exists for nothing else but to draw men into Christ, to make them little Christs. If they are not doing that, all the cathedrals, clergy, missions, sermons, even the Bible itself, are simply a waste of time. God became Man for no other purpose.
—*C. S. Lewis, Mere Christianity*

The church's primary function here on earth is to be a community of disciples who make disciples (or, as Lewis puts it, "little Christs"). This disciple-making mandate has to become front and center in all that we do and are.

Dietrich Bonhoeffer succinctly summarized our shared calling when he wrote, "Discipleship means adherence to Christ and, because Christ is the object of that adherence, it must take the form of discipleship."[72]

Yet too often discipleship has slipped off the radar of the church—and if we're honest, it's rarely on the radar of most Christians. Perhaps they feel ill equipped to disciple others well, or don't know how to create structures that will sustain disciple making, or are simply too busy doing everything else that they feel they're meant to be doing as a follower of Jesus. Our friend Bill Hull has commented that discipleship has become an extra, an add-on, like a pro athlete picking up an option on his contract.

Our goal in this book has been to give you some tools and much-needed encouragement in your journey of making disciples (and being

215

discipled). By describing the power of the Five Contexts and their strengths and weaknesses, we offer a framework for engaging with a variety of different discipleship opportunities. As you come with the right expectations into each of the contexts, you set yourself up for far more success in disciple making than you have ever known before.

Furthermore, the Five Contexts demonstrate that you don't have to be in a religious setting to make disciples. You can do it anytime and anywhere, and have fun at the same time! Jesus wants you to always be making disciples as an overflow of your lifestyle so that discipleship becomes deeply ingrained in your life.

The church's primary function here on earth is to be a community of disciples who make disciples of Jesus.

Early in the book we shared our belief that humanity's ability to connect and build relationships in the different contexts is something God has hardwired into us. The "rules" for relating in the different contexts somehow reflect and draw upon our intrinsic natures—when we are healthy, we intuitively operate by these rules. Yes, there are cultural nuances, but the general rules still apply around the world.

Therefore it follows that we should be able to take these principles and apply them at work, at school, in our neighborhood, and so on. Even if we are not at liberty to talk about being a Christian, we can take these ideas and start to knead them into the places where we have some influence, using them to shape our leadership.

For instance, think about leadership in the workplace:

- What would be different about staff meetings in the Social and Personal Contexts?
- If you identified a corporate blind spot in your organization, at what size of gathering would you address it?
- When a team member is underperforming, what context would provide the best environment for speaking to them with candor?
- In which context would your "heroes" be honored and valued?
- How would you reward your teams in different contexts?

Even if you are not in a position of leadership at the moment, you do have leadership influence and can start to adjust your interactions accordingly.

TRANSITIONING BETWEEN CONTEXTS

Sometimes a group you are leading will begin to shift from one context to another—such as a group in the Personal Context that is intentionally growing into the Social Context as a missional community. The tension comes in that in-between space between the contexts. For instance, let's say you now have fifteen people. How should your gathering times be formatted?

Our advice here is to "act up" to the size you want to be. In other words, operate as if you are already the size you aspire to be. So even if you have just fifteen adults and kids present, act as if there are twenty-five of you. Thus you won't sit in one circle sharing prayer requests (Personal Context activity) but instead will subdivide into smaller groups to facilitate that part of your time together.

In "acting up," you are setting the tone for how the group will operate when it's larger. Intuitively the fifteen will think to themselves, "There is room here for newcomers without a huge cost to those already in the group (including me!)." Or you might "act down," by breaking a large small group of sixteen people into smaller groups of four or eight when you gather.

Bear in mind that in some situations you might be better off multiplying rather than simply growing larger. Thus a missional community of forty-five that meets in a home could well find it simpler to split into two or three new groups and grow from there, rather than trying to manage becoming more of a congregation-sized gathering. The latter is not wrong to do but is far more complex, and so the multiplication route often can be easier to pull off than you might realize.

A bridgehead to this multiplication is to regularly subdivide your missional community during your times together. For instance, every time you want to pray together, have people break into smaller units to do this. You might find that, over time, some of these subsets start to form an identity of their own that eventually leads to a new missional community.

Even if that doesn't occur, you will have successfully spawned healthy small groups within your wider community.

HIGHLY URBAN CULTURES

As we consider how to transition between different contexts, further questions do arise. While we believe the sociology behind the Five Contexts provides an excellent framework for thinking about discipleship, the contexts do need to be used wisely. They are a means to an end, not an end in themselves.

Consequently, they may need to be tweaked in certain settings. For instance, while in the suburbs the numbers we use to measure the size of each context are fairly accurate, in the setting of a highly urbanized city, the numbers seem to run a little high.

Our friend Caesar Kalinowski, based in the heart of New York City, has found that his discipleship team can make the Five Contexts work with lower numbers of people. Thus the Social Context kicks in at around sixteen or seventeen people, while the Personal Context works best in the low single digits. Caesar explains that in the new urban world, the defining relationships are among friends rather than families, and people live incredibly busy lives, coming home frazzled after long workdays and stressful commutes to tiny apartments that give little room to breathe. Groups simply end up being smaller as that is what works pragmatically, although they are still defined by the key outcomes we have been using throughout this book (thus, for instance, the Social Context groups are shaped by community, mission, and practice). So again, we see the importance of having clear outcomes that can be applied flexibly.

Even with such busy lifestyles, people still desperately want (and need) community, but they need help in building it because their margin for mission is so low. Thus Caesar and his team have invested a lot of effort into creating simple Social Context on-ramps in local neighborhoods: community Happy Hours, progressive dinners, joint workouts at the gym, and more. In providing these opportunities for people to connect relationally, Caesar is taking the principles of the Five Contexts and, like a good missionary, applying them in the place where he is called to make disciples.

BARRIERS TO EMBRACING A DISCIPLE-MAKING CULTURE

Of course, this context-savvy awareness is not always as smooth sailing as it can sound! For those of you who are church leaders, be aware that the farther you head toward prioritizing a disciple-making culture that operates in each of the Five Contexts, the greater the challenges you will face. This is not an easy shift to make, and you will encounter opposition—from the enemy, from those who enjoy being enabled to live as Christian consumers, from those who fear loss of power, and, if you are honest, from your own internal dissonance.

To tear down all of those barriers is beyond the scope of this book (although we have tackled quite a few of them), but you may find it helps simply to write down a number of them. We suggest that you, along with your leadership team, study the starter lists in the sidebar, add to them, and identify which barriers are the most pressing in your context.

Ask those leaders assembled with you to individually review these lists and note the top three barriers that prevail in your context. Then see if the whole group can prioritize the lists and then openly discuss solutions and strategies to implement the solutions.

To be forewarned gives you room to become forearmed so that you can discuss how to tackle the key issues. Often the external barriers are easier to resolve, and so we especially must address internal opposition to a disciple-making culture, beginning with our own hearts.

GIVE PEOPLE SIMPLE STEPS

As you seek to build a disciple-making culture, whether at church, at your workplace, or in your neighborhood, you need to give people simple steps to succeed in the different contexts. Here are some quick next moves for a variety of classic questions that will be posed:

- Many people are so ingrained into the Public Context, with its anonymity, that they don't know how to interact socially with others. At certain points we have had to provide training for people in what might be called social skills—this is how

12 INTERNAL BARRIERS TO EMBRACING A DISCIPLE-MAKING CULTURE

1. Indifference to what God is saying and doing
2. Refusal to repent of the sins that are undermining the Western church
3. Job insecurity: "Will I be fired if I pursue discipleship over consumerism?"
4. General fear of the unknown
5. "I was never (properly) discipled, so how can I disciple others?"
6. My ego might be unhealthily tied to success in the current model
7. The challenge of choosing to go deep and not just wide
8. Fear that things will get messy and there will be unexpected results
9. "I won't be able to be in complete control or micromanage."
10. "I like my alone time and have stopped enjoying being with people for long."
11. The personal cost for me and my family
12. Unwillingness to become more vulnerable

12 EXTERNAL BARRIERS TO EMBRACING A DISCIPLE-MAKING CULTURE

1. The unbridled busyness of people
2. The prioritization of other things (such as sports) over Christian community
3. The history of our church, including her inherited "baggage"
4. The power of consumerism within our culture (especially in the suburbs)

5. "How will we sustain the existing financial engine of our church?" (or "How will we pay off the colossal building loan?")

6. The flighty nature of Christian consumers: "If I come on too strong, they'll leave our church."

7. "Many Christians don't really want to be discipled, let alone make disciples."

8. A shortage of leaders who "get it" and want to support the shift to a disciple-making culture

9. "I'm held accountable mostly for things unrelated to disciple making."

10. Current success: "We do a great job at what we already do."

11. The demands of current ministries on time, attention, and resources

12. Lack of margin for mission in the system

you welcome someone new, this is how you host a missional community meal, these are some tips for including families with children.

• For those who are nervous about committing to a new group, and in particular a missional community, we would encourage you to allow people to test out a group to see if it is a good fit for them. Give people explicit permission to sample a group or two. In the long run, it will build far higher commitment. You could also encourage missional communities to meet in a third space sometimes, such as a restaurant, park, or place of service, which for some will be easier to enter than an unknown person's home.

• For those who feel that they don't have time to live as we are recommending (in other words, to commit deeply enough with a group of others so that disciples are made), there is a very simple response. In essence the answer is that making disciples and living on mission generally should happen where you are already doing

life. If you go to school, make disciples at school. If you love your
neighborhood, live like a missionary in that environment. If you
are called to disciple your work colleagues, act as an ambassador
for Jesus in all your interactions. (For more on this, go back to
chapter 7.)

- For those who wonder whether their kids can join in and
  be (imperfect) kids, remind them that it is worth the effort!
  Again, we tackled this in chapter 7, but we know from personal
  experience that your children won't sit still like robots! And, more
  deeply, you long to see them discipled into the knowledge of the
  truth that is found in Jesus. The Five Contexts help us understand
  how different aspects of the journey of discipleship take place in
  different spaces, and in particular how the Social Context is an
  ideal size for folding children into a sustainable community life
  centered on Jesus.

- So many people today need counsel on how to operate graciously
  on social media. Those you disciple must grasp that social media
  is a Public Context environment and thus is not an appropriate
  setting for sounding off on pet peeves or lobbing bombs from a
  distance. You can help others grow in maturity in this area by
  using the Five Contexts to clarify social media's actual setting.

- Others need help balancing what is sometimes called the
  "brownies and Bible study" axis! If you only sit and eat brownies,
  where is the yardstick for truth? Instead, you are simply spouting
  off your opinions with little accountability. Challenge is part of
  the Personal Context—if you hang out only with those who agree
  with you, is that really an expression of a community of world-
  changing love? Meanwhile, others are only Bible and no brownies
  (which represent grace). Everyone needs space for an unfiltered
  release of emotions, knowing that they will be loved and called
  into a better spot. To pretend everything is perfect is not real and
  ultimately is harmful, because when hard times and tragedies
  strike, you need relationships of grace to see you through.

- Remember that language and vocabulary are important, and the larger your church, the clearer and tighter it will need to be. A shared language of discipleship bonds us together, communicates key values, helps measure key goals, and shows how we understand success.

- Also, recognize that growing in maturity as a disciple of Jesus involves submitting to being part of a group bigger than you (including with your money). Some believers love the Personal Context but are not accountable to anything bigger than themselves. Someone hurt them at some point, so now they buck the Public Context and thus miss out on the humility of setting their story within the grander sweep of what the Lord is doing in a specific place at a specific time. By giving a clear and positive explanation of why you hold weekend worship services—creating a place of inspiration, movementum, and preaching—you provide an honest and attractive rationale for gathering in the hundreds.

> A shared language of discipleship bonds us together, communicates key values, helps measure key goals, and shows how we understand success.

Discipleship is about following Jesus, hearing what he is saying and then obeying. Yet Jesus loves to take us on the journey by using those around us to help disciple us. To use biblical language, you belong to the body of Christ, and you are designed to play your part there, both giving and receiving.

Disciple making is an adventure—truly the most amazing adventure. What an awesome privilege to realize that Jesus' Plan A is to use each of us to help shape lives into his likeness! We are commissioned to be disciple-making disciples, playing our part in making disciples who in turn go and make disciples.

As I (Alex) have been writing this book, I've also been reading the *Wolf Hall* trilogy by Hilary Mantel. These Pulitzer Prize–winning novels have been widely acclaimed and even turned into a successful TV series.

The focus of them is the life of Thomas Cromwell, who served England's King Henry VIII during the 1530s.

Mantel is eager to show Cromwell as someone who apprenticed both men and women, enabling them to rise up and do more with and through their lives. Cromwell himself came from very humble origins, and that motivated his desire to give others opportunities to grow and flourish.

At one critical point near the end of *Wolf Hall*, Cromwell lies seriously ill but is fretting about who will do his work for the king. "A week passes. He is better and he wants work brought in but the doctors forbid it. How will it go forward, he asks, and Richard says, sir, you have trained us all and we are your disciples, you have made a thinking machine that marches forward as if it were alive, you don't need to be tending it every minute of every day."[73]

> As we go and make disciples, we are not making clones of ourselves but rather people who are committed to following Jesus wherever he takes them.

As we go and make disciples, we are not making clones of ourselves but rather people who are committed to following Jesus wherever he takes them. By emphasizing outcomes rather than tasks as the core measures of success in the different contexts, we equip people to follow Jesus in ways that build on their unique character and interests.

Our hope is that you will more confidently represent Jesus as he lives inside you in each of the Five Contexts! As you learn to recognize and embrace these different types of relationships, you will grow closer to God and be better able to disciple others in his name. You will have the joy of watching the kingdom advance exponentially in ways that are extraordinary to behold. To God be the glory!

Appendix One

"ONE ANOTHER" COMMANDS IN THE NEW TESTAMENT[75]

IN A WONDERFUL short essay, Jeffrey Kranz comments on the "one another" commands in the New Testament. He notes that these two words in English actually translate a single word in the original Greek, hence our made-up word "oneanothering" is entirely biblical! Kranz notes several key themes that emerge from the one hundred New Testament occurances of this word:

Unity: approximately 33 percent

1. Be at peace with one another (Mark 9:50)
2. Don't grumble about one another (John 6:43)
3. Be of the same mind with one another (Romans 12:16, 15:5)
4. Accept one another (Romans 15:7)
5. Wait for one another before beginning the Lord's Supper (1 Corinthians 11:33)
6. Don't bite or devour one another (Galatians 5:15)
7. Don't provoke or envy one another (Galatians 5:26)
8. Gently, patiently bear with one another (Ephesians 4:2)
9. Be kind, compassionate, and forgiving to one another (Ephesians 4:32)
10. Bear with and forgive one another (Colossians 3:13)
11. Strive to do good for one another, and don't repay wrong for wrong (1 Thessalonians 5:15)

12. Don't slander one another (James 4:11, 5:9)

13. Do confess sins to one another (James 5:16)

Love: again, approximately 33 percent

1. Love one another (John 13:34, 15:12, 17; Romans 13:8; 1 Thessalonians 3:12, 4:9; 1 Peter 1:22; 1 John 3:11, 4:7, 11; 2 John 5)

2. Humbly serve one another in love (Galatians 5:13)

3. Bear with one another in love (Ephesians 4:2)

4. Greet one another with a kiss of love (1 Peter 5:14)

5. Be devoted to one another in love (Romans 12:10)

Humility: around 15 percent

1. Honor one another above yourself (Romans 12:10)

2. Value one another as more important than yourself (Philippians 2:3)

3. Serve one another humbly in love (Galatians 5:13)

4. Wash one another's feet (John 13:14)

5. Don't be proud, but associate with one another regardless of social position (Romans 12:16)

6. Submit to one another, especially in household relationships (Ephesians 5:21)

7. Clothe yourselves with humility toward one another (1 Peter 5:5)

The remainder:

1. Do not judge one another, and don't put a stumbling block in the way of a brother or sister (Romans 14:13)

2. Greet one another with a holy kiss (Romans 16:16; 1 Corinthians 16:20; 2 Corinthians 13:12)

3. Husbands and wives shouldn't deprive one another of sexual relations (1 Corinthians 7:5)

4. Carry one another's burdens (Galatians 6:2)

5. Speak truthfully to one another (Ephesians 4:25)

6. Do not lie to one another (Colossians 3:9)

7. Encourage one another concerning the resurrection (1 Thessalonians 4:18)

8. Encourage and build up one another (1 Thessalonians 5:11)

9. Spur one another on toward love and good deeds (Hebrews 10:24)

10. Pray for one another for healing (James 5:16)

11. Offer hospitality to one another (1 Peter 4:9)

Appendix Two

APEST AND APOSTLES TODAY

THE EXISTENCE AND ROLE of the apostolic function in the post–New Testament church has been a matter of some debate down through the centuries! Our understanding is that we do have apostolic leaders who operate in a role similar to that of the original apostles, except none are foundational to the church, nor were they alive with the incarnate Christ. Paul writes about apostolic leaders in Ephesians 4:11–13: "So Christ himself gave the apostles, the prophets, the evangelists, the pastors and teachers, to equip his people for works of service, so that the body of Christ may be built up until we all reach unity in the faith and in the knowledge of the Son of God and become mature, attaining to the whole measure of the fullness of Christ."

Writing to the church, Paul designates five major functionary roles in the church: apostle, prophet, evangelist, shepherd ("pastor" in the NIV), and teacher, which gives us the acronym APEST. Those with the calling of apostle are shaped to be a blessing to their church through their pioneering, embracing of change, and ability to bring breakthrough in stuck situations.

How do we know that Paul was addressing those beyond the Twelve in this passage? The context of Ephesians points toward that understanding. In his well-known commentary, Markus Barth says that Paul's description of the church in Ephesians is different from descriptions in any other New Testament book, leading him to describe this section of Ephesians as "the Constitution of the Church."[76]

Not only does the church receive more prominence in Ephesians, but the church is not as localized—in terms of houses and district churches—as in other letters. Unlike Paul's usage of "church" in the letters of Galatians,

1 Corinthians, and Philippians, his usage in Ephesians describes the universal church. He never mentions any names or specific issues in Ephesians. As a result, many scholars believe it was a circular letter, intended for the region, not just for the city of Ephesus.

This is important for our discussion, because it means Paul's description of the five APEST functions in Ephesians was not limited to one time period or region. His letter is about the church in general. So when the goal of the apostle is to build up the body of Christ, this role applies to the universal church.

Furthermore, other passages in the New Testament describe individuals with the apostolic gifting other than the original Twelve. The Greek word for "apostle" (apostolos) is used eighty times in the New Testament. While most of these occurrences refer to the Twelve, three individuals are clearly designated by the word apostle: Barnabas in Acts 14:14, Epaphroditus in Philippians 2:25 (translated "messenger" in the NIV), and Jesus in Hebrews 3:1. These are important passages, for they point to apostles as people sent beyond the local church—people sent to take the gospel to new regions, to expand the kingdom of God beyond the local church.

What does an apostolic leader do in the church today? Alan Hirsch writes about apostolic leadership in *The Forgotten Ways*, commenting about the nature of this kind of apostle and the mission of God: "I can find no situation where the church has significantly extended the mission of God, let alone where the church has achieved rapid metabolic growth, where apostolic leadership cannot be found in some form or another. In fact, the more significant the mission impact, the easier it is to discern this mode of leadership."[77]

The church needs this type of "rapid metabolic growth" in America, as we have shown, and apostolic leadership is integral in achieving it. Alan Hirsch and Tim Catchim define the apostolic leader's primary role: "The apostle is tasked with the overall vigor, as well as extension of Christianity as a whole, primarily through direct mission and church planting. As the name itself suggests, it is the quintessentially missional ministry, as 'sentness' (Latin: mission) is written into it (apostello = sent one)."[78]

With regard to the Social Context, we have found it enormously helpful to recognize the different strengths that each of the five APEST functions bring to missional community life and leadership.

EXAMPLES OF MISSIONAL COMMUNITY PATTERNS

THIS APPENDIX ILLUSTRATES *through individual examples how unique mission contexts create different expressions of Up, In, and Out.*

1. FAMILIES WITH ELEMENTARY KIDS

Realize that a missional community made up of families with young children will feature a high level of noise, activity, and mess! Rather than trying to be King Canute commanding the tide to reverse direction, allow the mild chaos to be a source of creativity and fun.

Up—Unusual forms of worship will be embraced with enthusiasm, so you can try out all sorts of things that adults by themselves might find beneath their dignity! Movement is important and helpful, and in turn will make those moments of quiet and stillness all the more impacting. Then as you engage with the Bible (probably one with lots of interesting pictures), make sure that the children are able to truly share their insights—yes, some will be a bit silly, but others will be unwittingly profound.

In—Food will need to be of the mass-produced, easy-to-clean-up variety! This doesn't mean it can't be healthy, but probably this is not the occasion to fight that particular battle. The meal table provides a great opportunity for adults and children to mingle, especially as the conversation shifts to stories about school, families, and life, and learning from Jesus in those situations. In the best groups, children see the adults demonstrate that what they share is taken seriously and valued.

Out—While your primary focus is on reaching and drawing in other families with elementary-aged children, as a group you can find opportunities to serve in the wider world as a context for discipleship. For instance, consider adopting a needy family at Christmastime, organizing a work morning to clean up the grounds of the local elementary school, or collecting money for a good cause. Children are superb witnesses for Jesus, so as a group you can train each other in some evangelism skills as well as join in prayer for friends, neighbors, and family members.

2. A RESIDENTIAL HOME FOR THE ELDERLY

Often residential homes will be open to a group that wants to be a regular part of their community, since the danger of institutionalization is always present. One of the best things you can do is bring a new level of energy, love, and interest to life there. Don't forget to bring the kids—many older folks love having babies and children around and reminiscing about their own children's milestones.

Up—Hammering out some classic old hymns is a great approach, since most older people have at least a basic knowledge of some aspects of church culture. Likewise, using the King James Version of the Bible might well be a good move, especially for well-known verses and passages. When it comes to discussion, recognize that people might be reluctant to speak up—whether due to aging voices or to a generational desire to be courteous and not disagree with what has been shared.

In—While many older people have special dietary needs and will want to eat the regular meals served at the home, you can try planning some events that hark back to old times, such as a summer tea party featuring home-baked goods that resonate with their childhood experiences. In terms of building closeness, prayer requests can be shared around the tables and brought to the Lord in a brief time of prayer. Later if you are able to visit people in their rooms, you can pray together again, especially for sickness or more private concerns.

Out—While the vision is to impact every resident in that home, you can invite those who live there to join you in serving those outside of that place without leaving it! For instance, knitting baby wear for the local crisis pregnancy center, recording some of their stories from the past to be played in school social studies classes, or writing letters of encouragement to those incarcerated in a local juvenile correction facility. If possible, try to pick a place where other Christians are already serving so that what the folks in the residential home do adds to that ongoing witness. And for residents who are committed to Christ and willing to grow as intercessors, help collect specific prayer requests from all sorts of people, contexts, and ministry situations.

3. MEN'S GROUP

Often men will gather around a specific event or activity but will find it difficult to share personal information. The Social Context is an ideal size for men because they can chat and connect over a common task, and when they are ready they can share more openly and form a few deeper relationships.

Up—Invite guys to pause and be thankful for what they have. Encourage them to move beyond the obvious (family, money, health) and think more about their identities and destinies. Show how the Bible gives practical guidance and advice for living well, such as how to conduct themselves wisely in the workplace, how to be a good husband or father, or how to become a leader of integrity in their community.

In—Food is rarely a mistake here! No doubt pancakes and bacon or pizza and breadsticks will be a hit, but also consider creating a more memorable experience sometimes. Is anyone a genuine grill master, or can someone teach how to cook a great curry, or would anyone be willing to lead a wine tasting? When men are having fun and gaining new knowledge, all sorts of interesting relationships can take shape. When it's time to process life, encourage the men to form prayer trios as subsets of the bigger group.

Out—In middle age, the big challenge for men (especially in the middle class) is moving from a life of success to a life of significance. Helping them think through this shift is vital, as is finding a few key projects that you as a group can do that will make a difference. Whether it's as simple as doing repairs and yard work at the home of a struggling single mom, or tutoring kids who need help with schoolwork, or perhaps planning a bigger event where other men from workplaces and neighbor-hoods can be invited in, taking on a practical challenge together often has a way of bringing men closer together.

IN SUMMARY

Remember: these examples are intended to be descriptive rather than prescriptive! You will be able to think up better versions of these ideas and adapt these examples to your own place of mission. Nevertheless, the point is that we are to incarnate our faith into the specific contexts where God has placed us. By learning to love and understand the people we are reaching, we can better help them follow Jesus in more areas of their lives.

NOTES

1. See Jim Putman and Bobby Harrington with Robert Coleman, *DiscipleShift: Five Steps That Help Your Church to Make Disciples Who Make Disciples*, Exponential Series (Grand Rapids: Zondervan, 2013).

2. This definition and the basis for it is taken from the book by Bobby Harrington and Josh Patrick, *The Disciple Makers Handbook* (Grand Rapids: Zondervan, 2016).

3. The participles in vv. 19–20 are subordinate to the command "make disciples" and explain how disciples are made: by "baptizing" them and "teaching" them obedience to all of Jesus' commandments. The first of these involves the initiation into discipleship, and the second focuses on the lifelong task of sanctification or obedience. See Craig Bloomberg, *Matthew: An Exegetical and Theological Exposition of Holy Scripture*, The New American Commentary (Nashville: Broadman and Holman, 1992), 431.

4. Bobby Harrington and Josh Patrick, *The Disciple Makers Handbook* (Grand Rapids: Zondervan, 2016).

5. Bobby shows how discipleship works in the home in a book that he co-wrote with his son, Chad Harrington, and Jason Houser. See *Dedicated: Training Your Children to Trust and Follow Jesus* (Grand Rapids: Zondervan, 2015).

6. This theme is traced out well by two authors. Writing from a Calvinistic perspective is David Platt, *Follow Me: A Call to Die. A Call to Live* (Carol Stream, Ill.: Tyndale House, 2013). Writing from an Arminian perspective is Robert Picirilli, *Discipleship: The Expression of Saving Faith* (Nashville: Randall House, 2013).

7. For more on the biblical response to Jesus and his Gospel, see Bill Hull, *Conversion and Discipleship: You Cannot Have One without the Other* (Grand Rapids: Zondervan, forthcoming [2016]).

8. Dallas Willard, *The Divine Conspiracy* (San Francisco: HarperCollins, 1998), 299.

9. John Wimber, *Everyone Gets to Play*, ed. Christy Wimber (Boise: Ampelon, 2008), 14.

10. John Ortberg, *The Life You've Always Wanted* (Grand Rapids: Zondervan, 1997), 18.

11. Richard Foster, *Celebration of Discipline: The Path to Spiritual Growth*, rev. ed. (San Fransisco: HarperSanFrancisco, 1998), 8.

12. Willard, *Divine Conspiracy*, 303.

13. David Watson, *Discipleship* (London: Hodder and Stoughton, 1981), 19.

14. You can read more about this story in Jim Putnam, *Real Life Discipleship* (Colorado Springs: NavPress, 2010), 36.

15. Bobby worked with Bill Hull on a point that is similar to this but is framed a little differently in the book *Evangelism or Discipleship: Can They Effectively Work Together?* (Exponential Resources, 2014), Kindle ed.

16. See N. T. Wright, *Simply Good News: Why the Gospel Is News and What Makes It Good* (San Francisco: HarperOne, 2015).

17. Set theory originally developed in mathematics in the 1870s and was first applied to missiology (the theology of how we go and live on mission) a century later. See Paul G. Hiebert, *Sets and Structures: A Study of Church Patterns* (Grand Rapids: Baker Book House, 1979), 217–27.

18. Paul Meshanko, *The Respect Effect* (New York: McGraw-Hill, 2013), 55.

19. Putman, *Real Life Discipleship*, 35.

20. Joseph Myers, *The Search to Belong* (Grand Rapids: Zondervan, 2003).

21. Edward Hall, *The Hidden Dimension* (Garden City, NY: Doubleday, 1966).

22. Myers, *Search to Belong*, 36.

23. I shared an early version of this thinking in Mike Breen and Alex Absalom, *Launching Missional Communities* (Pawleys Island, SC: 3DM, 2010), 42.

24. The following graphics are available to be downloaded at *discipleship.org*.

25. See Myers, *Search to Belong*, 46.

26. Ibid., 37.

27. Ibid., 36.

28. Hall, *Hidden Dimension*, 162.

29. Myers, *Search to Belong*, 44.

30. Foster, *Celebration of Discipline*, 199.

31. We first encountered the word *movementum* in Alan Hirsch and Dave Ferguson, *On the Verge: A Journey into the Apostolic Future of the Church* (Grand Rapids: Zondervan, 2011).

32. Breen and Absalom, *Launching Missional Communities*, 44.

33. Rodney Stark, *The Rise of Christianity* (San Francisco: HarperCollins, 1997), 7.

34. James D. G. Dunn, *Word Biblical Commentary: Romans 9–16* (Dallas: Word, 1988), 38b: 891.

35. Ibid., 38b: 898.

36. Roger Gehring, *House Church and Mission* (Peabody, MA: Hendrickson, 2004).
37. For more on this, check out the excellent chapter in Myers, *Search to Belong*, 119.
38. We use this language because it is an umbrella term for all of our various groups.
39. Neal McBride, "The Small Group Letter," *Discipleship Journal* 59 (September/October 1990).
40. For more information on this definition, see Putman and Harrington, *DiscipleShift*.
41. Malcolm Gladwell, *The Tipping Point* (Boston: Little, Brown & Co., 2002), 173.
42. "George Whitefield," *Christianity Today*, last modified August 8, 2008, accessed March 24, 2015, *http://www.christianitytoday.com/ch/131christians/evangelistsandapologists/whitefield.html*.
43. Stephen Tomkins, *John Wesley: A Biography* (Grand Rapids: Eerdmans, 2003), 199.
44. Kenneth J. Collins, *The Theology of John Wesley: Holy Love and the Shape of Grace* (Nashville: Abingdon Press, 2007), 250.
45. See Wesley Hill, *Washed and Waiting: Reflections on Christian Faithfulness and Homosexuality* (Grand Rapids: Zondervan, 2010), and Rosaria Butterfield, *The Secret Thoughts of an Unlikely Convert* (Pittsburgh: Crown & Covenant, 2014).
46. Jim Putman et al., *Real-Life Discipleship Training Manual: Equipping Disciples Who Make Disciples* (Colorado Springs: NavPress, 2010).
47. See Mike Breen's popular internet article on the need for discipleship to drive missional communities, "Why the Missional Movement Will Fail," http://www.disciplingculture.com/why-the-missional-movement-will-fail/, accessed August 20, 2015.
48. Because the level of intimacy is so deep, cross-gender groups are deemed unwise in most situations.
49. Neil Cole, *Search and Rescue: Becoming a Disciple Who Makes a Difference* (Grand Rapids: Baker, 2008).
50. Robby Gallaty, *Growing Up: How to Be a Disciple Who Makes Disciples* (Bloomington, IN: CrossBooks, 2013).
51. Randy Pope, *Insourcing: Bringing Discipleship Back to the Local Church*, Leadership Network Innovation Series (Grand Rapids: Zondervan, 2013), Kindle ed., locations 2301–2303.

52. Tara-Leigh Cobble, *Mile Deep: A Practical Guide to Discipleship Groups* (2014).

53. Find out more about these groups by going to *sites.google.com/site/dgroups1219/*.

54. For more on how parents disciple their children, see Jason Houser, Bobby Harrington, and Chad Harrington, *Dedicated: Training Your Children to Trust and Follow Jesus* (Grand Rapids: Zondervan, 2015).

55. Almost every in-depth analysis of the state of discipleship in the church today points to the supreme need for people to get into the Word of God and apply it to their lives. See Eric Geiger Michael, *Transformational Discipleship: How People Really Grow* (Nashville: B&H Publishing Group, 2012), Kindle ed., locations 910–918. Bill Hybels summarizes the results of the Willow Creek REVEAL Study (a large-scale survey to assess congregations' spiritual maturity): "We learned that the most effective strategy for moving people forward in their journey of faith is biblical engagement. Not just getting people into the Bible when they're in church—which we do quite well—but helping them engage the Bible on their own outside of church." Hybels is quoted in Greg Hawkins and Cally Parkinson, *Move: What 1,000 Churches Reveal about Spiritual Growth* (Grand Rapids: Zondervan, 2011), Kindle ed., locations 71–72.

56. See David Buehring's excellent work, *The Jesus Blueprint: Rediscovering His Original Plan for Changing the World* (Oviedo, FL: Higher Life Publishing, 2012).

57. *Spurgeon's Sermons*, vol. 28, electronic ed. (Albany, OR: Ages Software, 1998).

58. "Quotes by Dwight Lyman Moody (1837–1899)," last modified October 1, 2013, accessed March 24, 2015, *http://www.jesus-is-savior.com/Great%20Men%20of%20God/dwight_moody-quotes.htm*.

59. Alister McGrath shows the importance of communal Bible study and how to do it in our world today. See McGrath, *A Passion for Truth: The Intellectual Coherence of Evangelicalism* (Downers Grove, IL: InterVarsity Press, 1996).

60. This is Dann Spader's language from the times he and Bobby have talked and worked together.

61. Dave Ferguson and Jon Ferguson, *Exponential: How You and Your Friends Can Start a Missional Church Movement* (Grand Rapids: Zondervan, 2010), 63.

62. Donald Miller, *Scary Close: Dropping the Act and Finding True Intimacy* (Nashville: Nelson Books, 2014).

63. In addition to the books listed in "Additional Resources for the Divine Context" on page 214, see Richard J. Foster, *Sanctuary of the Soul: Journey into Meditative Prayer* (Downers Grove, IL: IVP Books, 2011); Dallas

Willard, *Hearing God: Developing a Conversational Relationship with God*, expanded ed. (Downers Grove, IL: IVP Books, 2012); John Ortberg, *Soul Keeping: Caring for the Most Important Part of You* (Grand Rapids: Zondervan, 2014); see also *www.johnortberg.com*.

64. Willard, *Divine Conspiracy*, 353–54.

65. *The Spirit of the Disciplines: Understanding How God Changes Lives* (San Francisco: HarperSanFrancisco, 1990), 98.

66. Jack Deere, *Surprised by the Power of the Spirit* (Grand Rapids: Zondervan, 1996), 171.

67. See more on this point in our friend Todd Wilson's book, *More: Find Your Personal Calling and Live Life to the Fullest Measure* (Grand Rapids: Zondervan, 2016).

68. Dallas Willard, *Hearing God: Developing a Conversational Relationship with God* (Downers Grove, IL: IVP Books, 2012).

69. For more on prayer journaling, see Wayne Cordeiro, *The Divine Mentor* (Bloomington, MN: Bethany House, 2007).

70. Michael Frost and Alan Hirsch, *The Faith of Leap* (Grand Rapids: Baker Books, 2011), 81.

71. Eric Metaxas, *Bonhoeffer: Pastor, Martyr, Prophet, Spy* (Nashville: Thomas Nelson, 2011), 268.

72. Dietrich Bonhoeffer, *The Cost of Discipleship* (New York: Touchstone, 1995), 59.

73. Hilary Mantel, *Wolf Hall* (New York: Henry Holt, 2009), 504.

74. Jeffrey Kranz, "All the 'One Another' Commands in the NT," *OverviewBible.com*, last modified March 9, 2014, accessed March 24, 2015, http://overview bible.com/one-another-infographic/, used by permission of the author.

75. Markus Barth, *Ephesians: Introduction, Translation, and Commentary on Chapters 1–3*, Anchor Bible, vol. 34 (Garden City, NY: Doubleday, 1960), 32–36.

76. Alan Hirsch, *The Forgotten Ways* (Grand Rapids: Brazos, 2007), 151.

77. Alan Hirsch and Tim Catchim, *The Permanent Revolution* (San Francisco: Jossey-Bass, 2012), 10.

A personal message from Alex

If you're applying the 5 Contexts, I'd love to hear from you!

Send your best story,
or most pressing question,
to my personal email address:
alex@dandelionresourcing.com

Also check out
www.dandelionresourcing.com
- that's my initiative to empower
leaders just like you!

DANDELION

Empowering Disciple-Making Leaders